William Joseph Seymour Black Father of The Twentieth Century Pentecostal/Charismatic Movement

Rufus G. W. Sanders, Ph.D.

Copyright © 2003 by Rufus G. W. Sanders, Ph.D.
First Reprint: February 2003

William Joseph Seymour
by Rufus G. W. Sanders, Ph.D.

Printed in the United States of America

ISBN 1-591601-64-9

All rights reserved. No part of this publication may be reproduced or transmitted in any form or by any means without written permission of the author.

Unless otherwise indicated, Bible quotations are taken from the King James Version. Copyright © 1997 by Tyndale House Publishers, Wheaton, IL. 60189

Published by
Alexandria Publications
P.O. Box 883
Sandusky, OH 44870

Xulon Press
www.XulonPress.com

Xulon Press books are available in bookstores everywhere, and on the Web at www.XulonPress.com.

In memory of Bishop Morris E. Golder
and
For Dr. Art Glass

ACKNOWLEDGMENTS

This project began in 1969 at the National Youth Convention of the Pentecostal Assemblies of the World. In that year the meeting was held in Buffalo, New York. I heard a lecture on the history of the Pentecostal Assemblies of the World by Bishop Morris E. Golder of Indianapolis, Indiana. He mentioned the name of William J. Seymour, an obscure black man who was now forgotten, but who had actually given birth to the twentieth-century Pentecostal Movement worldwide. From that moment on I feverishly engaged my energy into reconstructing the life of Seymour. Finally I have accomplished that dream.

I would like to thank the late Bishop Golder who supported my work throughout the years. He allowed me to interview him on numerous occasions. I dedicate this work to him. I am especially grateful to my dear friend and brother, Bishop C. Franklin Showell of Baltimore, Maryland. His sharp knowledge of early twentieth-century Pentecostal history and our many conversations helped to keep my interest alive through the years. His sharing with me of his memorabilia and his research have been most helpful and inspirational. I am indebted to Brenda Square of the Amistad Research Center at Tulane University in New Orleans, Louisiana, for her skill, interest and her boundless energy as a librarian-archivist. I am indebted as well to archivists at the Oral Roberts University Library, particularly the Spirit Room collection; the Los Angeles Public Library, the Butler Library at Columbia University in New York City, Tilden Memorial Library at Tulane University in New Orleans, the Ashland Theological Seminary Library, Ashland, Ohio, and the Bowling Green State University Library, Bowling Green, Ohio. A special thanks to Douglas C. Lynch, Manager of the Address Section, Division of Planning; and the Department of Metropolitan Development, City of Indianapolis, Indiana.

A number of people provided me with moral support along the way. Dr. Mel Robeck of Fuller Theological Seminary in Pasadena, California, generously listened to my thoughts and shared his research, concerns and thoughts. A very special thanks to my friend, Dr. Art Glass, the original curator of The Bonnie Brae Street House, who took the time to drive me all over Los Angeles while doing research whenever I was on the West Coast. His tremendous interest and zeal has kept the Azusa Street dream alive for all of us. To him I also dedicate this work.

I would like to acknowledge the people of the Japanese Cultural Community Center and the Little Tokyo Service Center in Los Angeles who treated me like a royal visitor while on a research trip to the site of the original Azusa Street Mission. A special thanks goes to my classmates and fellows at Columbia University who were part of the Association of Religious and Intellectual Life (ARIL) Fellowship. They listened to my work making valuable constructive criticism and comments.

At Bowling Green State University, thanks are given to my close friend and colleague, Kim Caldwell, who was a source of strength and inspiration at all times during the difficult days of Ph.D work. I want to thank Dr. Grant, the chair of my department for having the confidence and vision to see that both of my feet, in the secular and spiritual world needed to be used. Dr. Don McQuarie, the chair of my committee has been a good friend, mentor and teacher. His patience and enthusiasm about my work has provided encouragement, support and inspiration. His personal and professional interest in my work has been overwhelming.

Finally, I would like to acknowledge my mother, Lena M. Sanders, for her careful spiritual training, guidance, everlasting love and complete support. My brothers and sisters, who are always supportive of everything that I do; especially my little brother, Dr. Eugene Sanders, who is not only my apprentice, but who has also been my mentor. A special thanks to my extended family at the Emmanuel Temple Church. They have allowed me to live an extraordinarily good life. I want to especially thank my secretary, Olivia Rowe, who reads everything that I write, and a thank you is extended to my transcriber, Shannon Eskridge, who made my burden much lighter mentally as well as in actuality. To my sister-in-law and word processor, Phyllis Lipford, you are a God-send. And finally to my very special friend, my wife, Dr. Jo-Ann Sanders, thank you for sharing my life.

                                          Rufus G.W. Sanders
                                          Sandusky, Ohio
                                          September, 2000

PREFACE

In most discussions of early American Christianity, historians omit the active role of Blacks. Instead, they have chosen to emphasize the impact of White Christianity on African-Americans through the institution of slavery. However, this study proposes that historical Pentecostalism can be traced from the revivalism of the early Methodist and Baptist Churches to a one-eyed Negro man named William J. Seymour.

Most writers have attributed the founding of Pentecostalism to Charles Fox Parham, a White man who preached a Pentecostalized Wesleyanism doctrine. His teachings indeed helped to formulate what would eventually become the foundations of Pentecostal theology. However, it was from Seymour's ministry in a dilapidated mission on Azusa Street in Los Angeles, California, that the twentieth-century Pentecostal revival sprang. Parham's position as Seymour's father in this new-found faith seems clear, but it was the Azusa Street experiences birthed by Seymour's ministry that was foundational for most twentieth-century Pentecostal denominations. However, Seymour's contribution to this great revival has not been properly understood. Seymour, a descendent of enslaved Africans, generated a spiritual dynamism that changed the face of Christendom.

The omission of William J. Seymour as father of the twentieth-century Pentecostal movement by historians is challenged. This narrative suggests the omission was due in part to the influence of American racism on subsequent historical records.

CONTENTS

Chapter *Page*

INTRODUCTION 1

1. THE SIGNIFICANCE OF WILLIAM J. SEYMOUR 5

2 WILLIAM SEYMOUR:

   PREDECESSORS AND EARLY LIFE 17

3. THE MIDDLE YEARS 37

4. THE EXODUS 47

5. THE TRAILBLAZER OF PENTECOSTALISM 61

6. ON TO LOS ANGELES 75

7. AZUSA STREET 93

AN AFTERWORD 131

BIBLIOGRAPHY 133

Seymour as a young man. This photo appeared in "Life and Ministry of Seymour" by Larry Martin.

Behold, this dreamer cometh, come now therefore, and let us slay him, and cast him into one of the pits, and we will say: Some evil beast hath devoured him; and we shall see what will become of his dreams.

                                                         Genesis 37:19-20

INTRODUCTION
THE SIGNIFICANT ABSENCE OF WILLIAM SEYMOUR IN THE HISTORY OF THE PENTECOSTAL MOVEMENT: BACKGROUND INFORMATION

In a special January 22, 2000 edition, *Life* magazine listed the most significant one hundred events in American history of the last century. In this issue, *Life* reported the Azusa Street Pentecostal revival which occurred in Los Angeles in 1906 as the sixty-eighth most important event to happen in America in the twentieth century.

This revival was led by William Joseph Seymour, an obscure black preacher who had moved to Los Angeles after having been initiated in the doctrines of Pentecostalism in Houston, Texas, by Charles Fox Parham, who had declared in 1901 that speaking in tongues was a sign of Holy Spirit baptism. Seymour's Los Angeles ministry began in 1906, when his leadership of a house prayer meetings on Bonnie Brae Street brought him an enthusiastic following. The following months saw explosive growth in Seymour's ministry, as hundreds and then thousands of people packed the house and surrounding streets to hear him speak. Within two years he had founded the Apostolic Faith Mission on Azusa Street, leading a congregation of thousands of followers and sending missionaries to twenty-five countries all over the world. At a time when most American institutions, including churches, were rigidly segregated, Seymour's movement was remarkable for its interracial composition.

Seymour had taken Pentecostalism from being a radical brand of Wesleyanistic Methodism and turned it into a universal church of a new-found Christian faith. By the end of the twentieth century, Protestants and Catholics alike had embraced aspects of

Pentecostalism, complete with speaking in tongues, shouting, hand-clapping, swaying and other forms of worship that have a definite African flavor to them. The Azusa Street movement initiated by Seymour a century ago has revolutionized contemporary Christianity. Today, according to Life magazine, about a half billion people call themselves Pentecostal and Pentecostals worldwide outnumber Anglicans, Baptist, Lutherans and Presbyterians combined. However, despite the significance of his life and his enormous influence on the development of twentieth-century Christianity, the life of William Joseph Seymour has received little study by historians and cultural scholars. There has been little written about the life of this very important black father of the Christian Church.

This narrative is the cumulation of a personal interest of rather long incubation. It is the neglected story of one of the most important figures in twentieth-century American religious history. It is the story of one of America's great folk icons, William Joseph Seymour, who initiated the Pentecostal/Charismatic Movement. From its humble beginnings at the Azusa Street Mission, Seymour launched a worldwide movement that engaged American institutional racism. For a brief period in American history there was a movement that did not embrace the color line.

The importance of Seymour has been underestimated and his presence has been underrated. Students of American religious history now speak of "a post-Protestant America" because of the Pentecostal revival that occurred with William J. Seymour's Azusa Street Revival that began in 1906 (Raboteau, 1997). The Movement began quietly in a small insignificant black prayer group, glossolalia[1] being its most visible characteristic. The group mushroomed into a movement that helped to usher in the Pentecostal age in the twentieth-century. The growth of this movement was explosive, and its social implications were profound.

Seymour's greatness lay not only in his theological belief in the significance of glossolalia, but in the socially multi-cultural nature of the movement he built. His vision gave the church and the world a unique opportunity for racial healing and reconciliation across the color line. Tragically, white religious leaders of this time not only disregarded this prophet of multi-culturalism, but neglected the profound impact of his experiment in racial reconciliation.

This narrative documents the deliberate attempt by white historians to deny Seymour the title of Father of the twentieth-century Pentecostal/Charismatic Movement. This study takes exception to the dominant view that Seymour was simply one major character among many in the movement. By providing him with a history and pedigree, and by chronicling his life within the organizational context of Pentecostal history, a more accurate portrait emerges than generally has been available.

This study is based on available historical documentation, dissertations, and other secondary and primary source materials. The use of these materials makes possible an evaluation of Seymour's life in relation to the revival of twentieth-century American religion in the Pentecostal Movement.

Our people were emancipated in a whirl of passion, and then left naked to the mercies of their enraged and impoverished ex-masters.

W. E. B. DuBois (1910)

CHAPTER 1
THE SIGNIFICANCE OF WILLIAM J. SEYMOUR

William Joseph Seymour is not only the main architect of modern Pentecostalism, but he deserves the status of Father of the twentieth-century Pentecostal Movement. Even though he has been given recognition as a major formulator in the creation of this worldwide movement, in most historical accounts he is only given status equal with that of Charles F. Parham. However, upon close examination of the historical record, this one-eyed black man (Hollenweger, 1970) emerges as the true originator and Father of the Pentecostal movement. Parham planted the seed, but Seymour gave birth and later nurturing to the experience of Pentecostalism.

Just as the Protestant Reformation traces its doctrinal formation to the work of Martin Luther, the Pentecostal/Charismatic Movement must recognize Seymour, not just as one of the founders because he is more than just one of the players; he is the central figure (Paris, 1982). He is not merely the disciple of Parham (Camacho, 1986), he is the black founder of the twentieth-century worldwide Pentecostal Movement (Lovett, 1975; Hollenweger, 1970; Tinney, 1980). From his Azusa Street Mission came what theologians have referred to as the "third force"[2] in Christianity because of its enormous revolutionary impact on the Christian Church.

Beginning in April, 1906, Seymour's Los Angeles-based Apostolic Faith Mission became the epicenter of the Pentecostal Movement.[3] From the famous Azusa Street revival the Pentecostal Movement was ignited. In the language of Church historian Walter Hollenweger, "The origins of the Pentecostal Movement go back to this revival amongst these Negroes of

North America (Hollenweger, 1972, p.17). During the next several years, visitors came from across the United States and abroad to receive the Pentecostal experience. "Revivals sprang up in...Jerusalem, India, China, South America, and the islands of the sea (Burgess, McGee & Alexander, 1988, p. 781). All twentieth-century Pentecostal movements throughout the world thus trace their origins back to Azusa Street and consequently Seymour's ministry (Golder, 1973; Synan, 1975; Tinney, 1971). Seymour's Azusa Street Mission became a new model on which twentieth-century Christianity was to be built. From a social perspective it was a multi-racial and a multi-cultural movement. Given the fact that it occurred during the height of Jim Crowism, this experiment was thus of striking sociological significance. Seymour was the leader of a distinct social movement, one where there was, for the first time in American history, no color line (Nelson, 1981).

In 1900 another great American of color, William E.B. DuBois, prophetically warned America of a horrendous looming social ill that if not resolved would plague her throughout the century. That social ill was the problem of the color line (DuBois, 1969). Seymour's movement offered a solution to America's racial problem. His Azusa Street Mission provided a social vision of racial harmony. His vision was compelling even though it was rejected by society in general and the churches specifically. The impact of his ministry and its unique contribution to the struggle for racial equality may never be fully understood, but it certainly did not go unnoticed at the time. Charles F. Parham, upon his visit to the Mission, expressed his displeasure:

> Men and women, whites and blacks knelt together or fell across one another. Frequently, a white woman, perhaps of wealth and culture, could be seen thrown back into the arms of a big black nigger, and held tightly thus as she shivered and shook in a freak imitation of Pentecost. Horrible, awful shame... (Shumway, 1914, p. 178).

These comments suggest that for many white religious leaders racial reconciliation was not considered to be an appropriate sign of God's pleasure. In fact, as far as Parham was concerned, race mixing was against the plan of God and therefore would not be tolerated in the Pentecostal church. Additionally, Parham (1993), writing about Seymour, noted: "...he may be credited with providing the vision of the color-blind congregation... ." His was a radical experiment that ultimately failed because of the inability of whites to allow for a sustained role for black leadership (Burgess, 1988, pp. 780-781).

Not until the life of Seymour and his significance to Christian history began to be explored in the late 1950's and early 1960's, did mainstream Christianity begin to accept Pentecostalism. C. Brumback (1961) documented in *Life A River* and *A Sound From Heaven* the contributions of Seymour. His writings aroused the curiosity of historians. These studies encouraged the acceptance of Pentecostalism into mainstream Christianity (Hamilton, 1972; Handy, 1977). Prior to Brumback's essay, a history of Christianity written by the highly respected author Kenneth Scott Latourette (1953) had summarized the entire Pentecostal Movement and yet never mentioned the name Seymour. Though Pentecostalism was a phenomenon widely known to theologians and religious scholars, it was generally neglected as part of the history of Christianity. As far as black Pentecostals were concerned, they were rarely mentioned. Lecturing at New York's Union Theological Seminary, the famous theologian, Dietrich Bonhoeffer, referred to black Pentecostals as the "stepchildren" (Lovett, 1978) of the church.

American racism disallowed the honor of "Father" of the Pentecostal movement to be bestowed on William J. Seymour. Thus the literature on Pentecostalism has failed to recognize that every ritual and practice of Pentecostalism had a precedent in African-American traditional religion and as the movement took shape specifically in an African American milieu. References to Seymour's contributions written by mainstream academics are often given from a "tongue-in-cheek" perspective. Historians that mention Seymour and Azusa Street often do so in a brief and poorly articulated manner. Historical accounts of the life of

Seymour are sparse. A dissertation about his life was completed by Douglas Nelson (1981) at the University of Birmingham, England, but no in-depth research has been done by American scholars. With the exception of the writings of Robeck (1993), Synan (1975) and Tinney (1971, 1978), Seymour is mentioned only in a cursory manner in pieces on Pentecostalism.[4] Rather than expand on the work of Nelson (1981), most writers simply use Nelson to verify Seymour's existence, subsequently trivializing his contributions to the initiation of the Pentecostal Movement. Nelson's dissertation primarily explored Seymour's life after 1900, leaving his formative years, 1870-1900, largely unexplored. Nelson suggested this was not an oversight on his part, but resulted from the lack of primary source material upon which to base a more complete treatment. Nelson has done an epochal job in writing about Seymour's later life. While acknowledging the paucity of primary research materials, I have uncovered primary sources from oral interviews with several still-living members of Seymour's church, county records, grave sites, marriage certificates, and slave records. These materials make possible both a more complete biography of Seymour and a more detailed discussion of the multi-cultural Azusa Street Revival.

Pentecostalism: Historical Origins

As Americans moved toward a new century, there was a frenzy within Christendom that centered around the apocalyptic end of time. In 1885, the famous evangelist D. L. Moody was in the forefront of a movement to evangelize the world by 1900. Daniels (1877) reported that at the Annual Northfield Conference organized by Moody, Pierson cited statistics that showed the plausibility of completing the Great Commission[5] by the end of the century. Moody was so moved that he jumped to his feet and asked the Conference, "How many of you believe this can be done? The crowd roared its approval and Moody appointed a committee to draft a document to promote the idea" (Daniels, 1877). Though the plan never was actually drawn up, the fervor of such a dream became the fire that lit Pentecostal candles all over

America. Moody stated in a sermon preached during this time, "...I looked on this world as a wrecked vessel. God has given me a life boat; and said to me, 'Moody, save all you can' ... " Daniels, 1877, p. 67).

Charles Parham and the Topeka Revelation

Topeka, Kansas, generally is considered the official place of origin of the twentieth-century Pentecostal Movement Quebedeaux, (1976). Paris (1982) has summarized Parham's and Seymour's role in Pentecostal history as follows:

> Parham's school and teaching achieved wide spread popularity, but it was due to the famous Azusa Street Revival..., the central figure being W. J. Seymour. It is the events in Topeka in December of 1900 that becomes a catapult for the worldwide Pentecostal Revival Movement (Paris, 1982, p. 23).

It was in Topeka that Parham reported that the following events had occurred at his Bethel Bible College and Faith Healing home that he started in 1898:

> In December of 1900 we had our examination upon the subject of repentance, conversion, consecration, sanctification, healing and the soon coming of the Lord. We had reached in our studies a problem -- what about the second chapter of Acts? ...I set the students at work studying out diligently what was the Bible evidence of the baptism of the Holy Ghost (Dayton, 1987; Ewart, 1975; Synan, 1975).

The Topeka revelation posited the early and lasting component of the twentieth-century Pentecostal dogma: tongue speaking. The key term mentioned in Parham's above account is Bible evidence, in Parham's view, that speaking in tongues represented validation that a person had been filled with the Holy Spirit. To the early Pentecostals this was consistent with the recorded example of Holy Spirit baptism cited in the books of Acts and Joel.

Late in the evening of January 1, 1901, at a prayer meeting in Topeka, Kansas, Ms. Agnes Ozman reportedly began to speak in the Chinese language, becoming the first person of record to have received the spirit baptism in the United States (Burgess, 1998; McGee, 1967; Nichol, 1966; Quebedeaux, 1976). Ozman later stated the following:

> It was nearly 11:00 o'clock on the first of January when it came into my heart to ask that hands be laid upon my head, the Holy Spirit fell on me and I began to speak in tongues glorifying God ... It was as though rivers of living water were proceeding from my innermost being (Paris, 1983, p. 23).

Within a few days others at the Bible school, including Parham, received the baptism in the Holy Ghost and spoke in tongues, demonstrating that Pentecost[6] had returned. These phenomena also marked the emergence of a developing "Pentecostal" theology. Parham was not content to stop at the conclusion that speaking in tongues was the initial evidence of Holy Spirit baptism. In an attempt to equate these twentieth-century versions of tongues with the accounts in the Book of Acts, Parham argued that the tongues of Topeka could not be defined merely as glossolalia, but as xenolalia, a particular pattern in which one speaks in a known language that is unknown to the speaker (Horton, 1994).

Confident that all language barriers had been removed by the Holy Spirit, Parham attempted to launch a worldwide evangelistic revival. His views on this matter were expressed in an interview that later appeared in the Kansas City Times in February, 1901:

> The Holy Ghost knows all the languages of the world, and all we have to do is to yield ourselves wholly to God and the Holy Ghost and power will be given us so that we can have such control of our vocal chords, that we can enter any country on earth and talk and understand languages. The time is now at hand when we should all receive this gift of tongues (Goff, 1992, p. 28).

Portrait of Charles Fox Parham in ministerial robes. Photo appears in *The Life and Ministry of William J. Seymour* by Larry Martin.

Although Parham met with little success in launching an ongoing movement, he set into motion the idea of an initial evidential sign as an indication that one was filled with the Spirit of God. While Parham may have been one of the first twentieth-century religious leaders to experiment with tongues, it is now widely recognized by Pentecostal writers that modern Pentecostalism's main architect was actually Seymour (Hollenweger, 1970; Paris, 1982; Seymour, 1975; Tinney, 1980). Seymour is called the central figure in worldwide Pentecostal revival, the founder of a multicultural movement that shared his "new found gospel with whites" (Tinney, 1971; Paris, 1982; Richardson, 1980).

Father Seymour

The origins of Pentecostalism in the twentieth century lie within the doctrines that come from the Wesleyan-Holiness movements and from the black church in America (Hollenweger, 1972; Synan, 1961). The White influences on the movement have been recognized and well documented by Pentecostal historians. Unfortunately, though, they have discouraged, and even ignored, the formative and fundamental influences of Blacks in the development of the movement. Charles Fox Parham, Ambrose Tomlinson, Daniel S. Warner, John Alexander Dowie, Martin Knapp, Phineas Bresee, etc., have not only been recognized, but eulogized and glorified. But it is William J. Seymour, arguably the most influential of all the pioneers, who has generally been marginalized, denied, and even forgotten. The primary reason for this is that he was black and they were white.

It has been maintained by most Pentecostal historians that "Parham, must be regarded the founder, because he first formulated the Pentecostal theology linking tongues with the Holy Ghost baptism (Goff, 1988). Since this central theological corpus, which defines the movement, came through Parham; many call him father (Goff, 1988). It is Iain MacRoberts, writing for the book, *African- American Religion: Interpretive Essays in History and Culture*, who posits the truth, that it was not Parhamian theology which caused the movement to spread to fifty nations within two years of the Azusa Revival, or grow to its current size

F. W. Williams, one of the first to receive the Holy Spirit at Bonnie Brae Street. He started one of the first missions after Azusa Street in 1906, in Mobile, Alabama. He took the Pentecostal message throughout the South. Portrait taken from *The Life and Ministry of William J. Seymour* **by Larry Martin.**

of some 360 million believers worldwide (Raboteau, 1997; Barrett, 1988). It was the black experiential roots added by William J. Seymour, which provided the foundation for and the momentum for the movement (Nelson, 1981; Synan, 1971; Tinney; MacRoberts, 1988; Hollenweger, 1972).

Seymour brought to birth the Azusa Street revival and the worldwide Pentecostal movement. For decades after his death Seymour's role in the origin of the Pentecostal movement has been largely ignored, but in recent years, his position as catalyst of the worldwide movement is coming to light.

Pentecostal historian, Vinson Synan, has indicated, as the following chart demonstrates, that every Pentecostal church in the world can trace its origins directly or indirectly to Seymour's Azusa Street Mission (Nelson, 1981; Synan, 1971; Tinney, 1978).

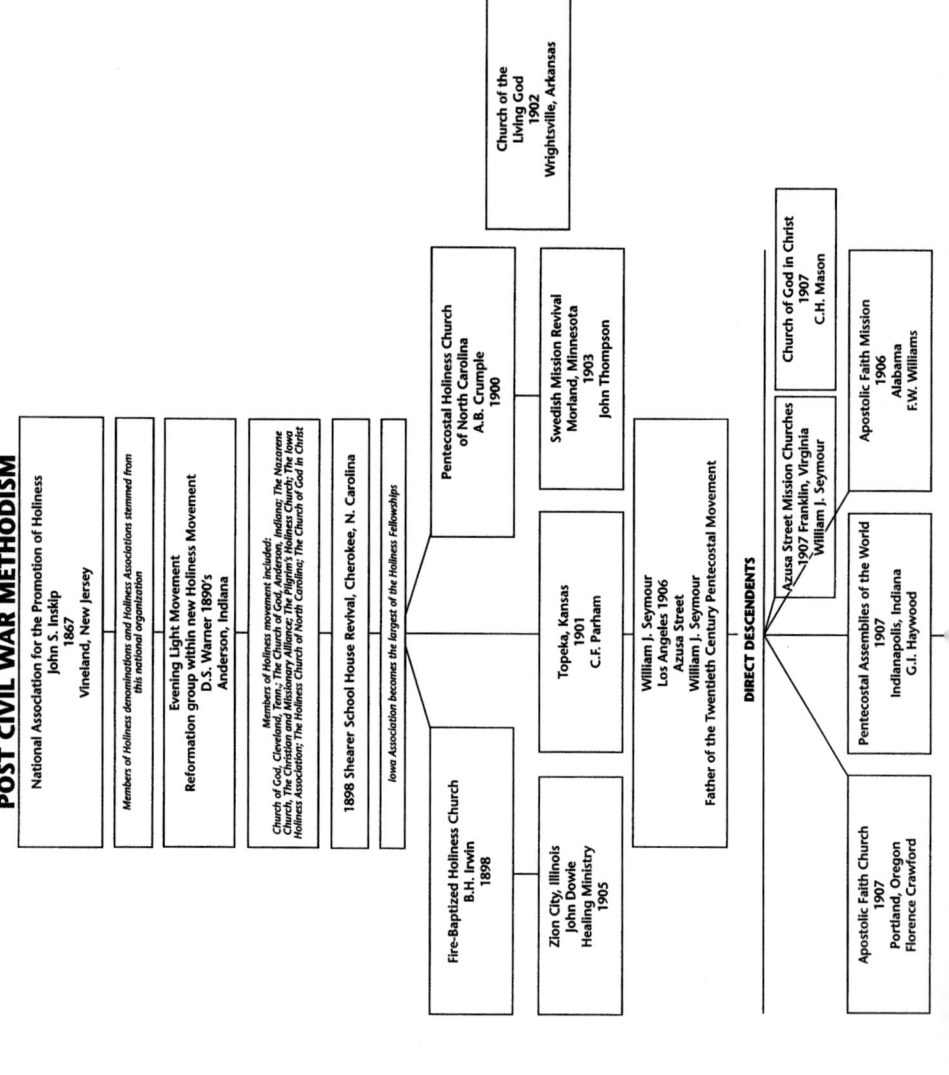

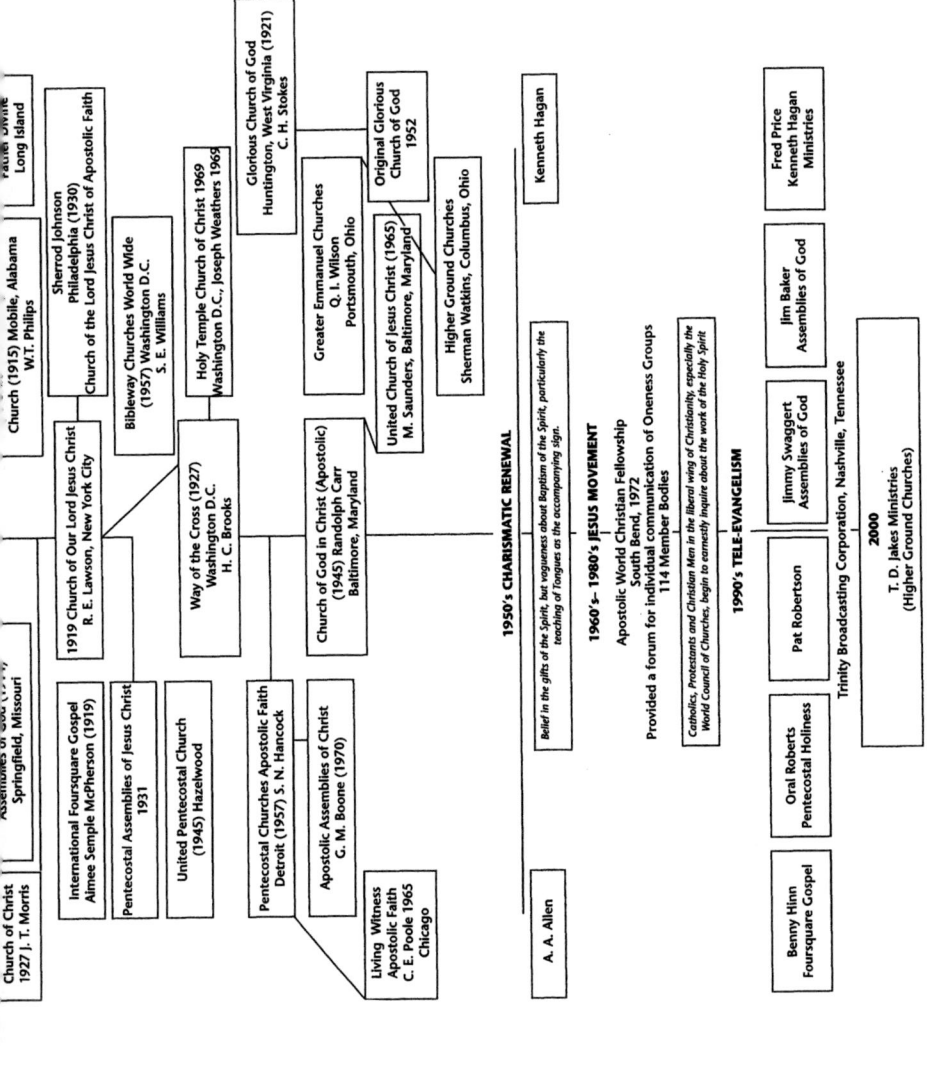

I believe in God who made of one blood all races that dwell on earth." "I believe that all men, black and brown and white, are brothers, varying through time and opportunity, in form and gift and features, but differing in no essential particular, and alike in soul and in the possibility of infinite development." "Especially do I believe in the Negro Race,"... "in the beauty of its genius, the sweetness of its soul and its strength in that meekness which shall yet inherit this turbulent earth." "I believe in Liberty for all men; the space to stretch their arms and souls, the right to breathe and the right to vote, the freedom to choose their friends, enjoy the sunshine and ride on the railroads, uncursed by color; thinking, dreaming, working as they will in a kingdom of God and love.

W. E. B. DuBois (1904)

CHAPTER 2
WILLIAM SEYMOUR: PREDECESSORS AND EARLY LIFE

Just west of New Orleans, the Crescent City as it is called, about ninety miles up the Mississippi River lies the sprawling Louisiana parish of St. Mary. Traveling due northwest on U.S. Highway 90 beyond the old Louisiana towns of Thibodaux, Houma, and Morgan City, one arrives at the center of the parish. There sits Centerville, present population of about five hundred. It is the birthplace of William Joseph Seymour (Nelson, 1981; Nickel, 1979; Tinney, 1978). The place remains virtually the same as it appeared one hundred years ago. There is still the one main street lined with aged oak and pine trees, giving rise to the town's colloquial name, Oak and Pine Alley (Guirard, 1968). The trees are resplendently arrayed in hanging Spanish moss, standing in front of white Corinthian-columned Greek revival mansions of a by-gone era (Spratling, 1927; Stahls, 1979). The place is almost constantly scented with the smells of tropical flowers and vegetation, as it is situated in the center of the warmest area of the Gulf Stream climate belt. The place is still a slow-paced paradise, a paradise in which the local citizens still date time in categories of floods, hurricanes, plagues or other natural calamities.

Seymour's Birthplace: A Brief History

The Bayou Teche, as the French called their rivers, flows alongside Centerville, turning south as it empties into Atchafalaya Bay. A Louisiana Chitimache Indian legend said that the Bayou was really the path of a giant serpent as it ceremoniously meandered a path between the Mississippi River and the Gulf of Mexico. Centerville sits in the middle of the delta formed by the nexus of the Mississippi River and the Gulf of Mexico. It is right in the heart of Cajun or Acadian country (Guirard, 1968).

The Teche country, as the area is called, is widely known for its beauty. The Bayou has an unending charm. For miles it runs like an ever-curling silver ribbon (Baker, 1982; Spratling, 1927). The red earth in which the oaks and pines sit shows through a tangle of vines and roots. The land is cut in seemingly irregular patterns of the various greens of fields bordered with luxurious foliage of all hues. The oaks provide an eerie appeal with their hanging canopy effect.

Some of the finest antebellum houses in the South are to be found in the parish of St. Mary. A large number of these historical treasures can still be seen along U.S. 90, which is also known as the Old Spanish Trail.[7]

In 1803, Napoleon sold the Louisiana Territory beyond the Mississippi River to the United States. In 1804 Congress passed an act dividing Louisiana into two territories --

> ...all that portion of country ceded by France to the United States under the name of Louisiana which lies South of the Mississippi River at the 33rd degree of latitude and to extend West to the Western boundary of said cession shall constitute a territory of the United States under the name of the territory of Orleans (Broussard, 1955).

President Jefferson appointed William C.C. Claiborne the new territory's first governor and in 1805 an act was passed by the legislative council at New Orleans for dividing the Orleans territory into counties. It was therefore divided into twelve parishes, Orleans, Germany Coast, Acadia, LaForche, Iberiaville, Point Coupee, Attakapas, Opelousas, Natchitoches, Rapides, Quachita and Concordia.

It was also decided that the county of Attakapas should include the parishes of St. Martin. On April 17, 1911, the county of Attakapas was further divided. From a portion of St. Martin Parish would come St. Mary Parish (Broussard, 1955). St. Mary's Parish would go on to play an important role in the history of the South. According to the Louisiana Landmark Society records, St. Mary's Parish has provided the state with four U.S. senators, four governors, and one chief justice of the state Supreme Court. St. Mary also was the early boyhood home of Jefferson Davis, President of the Confederacy (Louisiana Landmark Society Historic Guide to St. Mary Parish, 1965).

Although the original settlers were predominantly French and Acadian, by the early 1800's many people from Ireland, Germany, Holland, England, and other American states had found their way to St. Mary (Broussard, 1955). The Acadians, who had been driven from Nova Scotia by the British in 1755, were French colonists who had left their native land in 1604 and began the colonization of Acadia, as Nova Scotia was then called. In 1713 France deeded Acadia to England. Many years of unrest followed. Finally in 1755 the English governor of Canada issued an ultimatum to the Acadians: "Severe allegiance to the British crown and forsake your Catholic faith; or be expelled from Acadia...." (Guirard, 1968). Several thousand Acadians chose exile, and thus began "*LeGrand De'rangement*" (Guirard, 1968).

Their homes burned, their dead left behind, empty handed, destitute but defiant, they were herded into over-crowded ships. After weeks of suffering, these courageous Acadians, or Cajuns, as they became popularly known, were cast ashore in ports along the Atlantic Coast from Maine to Georgia (Nelson, 1981). They were displaced in arbitrary groups without regard to family ties or friendships. Extremely unhappy, the majority eventually made their way to Louisiana, then a French Colony, where their own language was spoken and their Catholic religion was practiced. Their descendants formed the major part of the population of Iberia, St. Mary and St. Martin Parish. All of these parishes lie in the part of southwest Louisiana known as the Evangeline Country. This area was immortalized in the poem, "Evangeline" by the American poet Henry Wadsworth Longfellow (Nelson, 1981). Longfellow wrote the poem in 1835, using a theme from the French-speaking Acadians.

St. Martinville, the heart of Cajun country, would become the "county seat" of Iberia Parish, birthplace of William J. Seymour's father, Simon (Nelson, 1981; Nickel, 1979; Tinney, 1978). One of the first public buildings to be built in the parish at St. Martinville was the courthouse. Famed for its architectural beauty, it was built by slave labor just before the Civil War (Guirard, 1968). One of the earliest judges to serve in this courthouse was Edward Simon (Guirard, 1968). He would eventually sit on the Supreme Court of the State of Louisiana. Following in his footsteps, his son also presided over the local court, as did a grandson and a great grandson (Guirard, 1968). Judge Edward Simon was born in 1827, in St. Mary Parish, but he actually lived in Iberia Parish at St. Martinville (Chambers, 1925; Perrin, 1891). He served the State of Louisiana as a Democrat (Chambers, 1925). He was a member of St. Peter's Roman Catholic Church (Perrin, 1891).

As fate would have it, during the days of Reconstruction a mulatto ex-slave born to the Simon family, known only as Simon, the father of William Joseph Seymour, would also serve as an appointed municipal judge and constable for a short period of time (Bergerie, 1961).

Simon, like other residents of the area, both black and white, was probably bilingual. At the least he would have understood French, because it was the official language of the area.[8] Cajun French predominated in the region until the 1920's, when it was banned from schools in a move toward assimilation (Clark, 1999). A story is told that perfectly explains the bilingual nature of the culture in the Cajun region of southwest Louisiana.

...you find a gentleman with an Irish name who speaks English as though he had just left the Foxborough St. Germain on the streets of St. Martinville, you attempt a conversation with the old colored man, a paralytic, who begs there and results are nil until a passer-by advises you go try French. Instantly he becomes valuable in that language (Bergerie, 1962, p.35).

While Centerville sits in the middle of the St. Mary Parish, it is also in the middle of the Mississippi delta region. In 1853 Centerville had a population of about two hundred citizens. It had a general store, a cypress lumber sawmill, a 350-ton capacity ice house, a general mercantile business, and several inns (Broussard,

1955). It also had a post office and was the "center" of sugar activity during the steamboat era. The town of Centerville was so named because it was once the "center" of railroad travel and the shipping point for this sugar-rich section of the Louisiana Teche country (Stahls, 1979).

St. Mary Parish and Centerville in particular were always vibrant and prosperous. This prosperity was largely due to the extensive cane cultivation in the parish and the existence of a large slave population. Slaves played an important and prominent role throughout the antebellum history of St. Mary Parish. Public auction of slaves were held frequently on the courthouse lawn and advertised beforehand in the planters' trade papers (Broussard, 1955). In these advertisements, many things were taken into consideration -- hands, age, disabilities, and handicaps. A husky healthy male slave might sell for as high as $1,200; while a weak and sickly one for as little as $200 (Broussard, 1955).

The life of slaves in St. Mary Parish, like everywhere else, was well regulated. The slave would rise in the dim pre-dawn light, with but a single noon-hour rest, toiling in the cane fields until night. Records indicate at least in St. Mary Parish there were no unusual or severe cases of mistreatment or overwork. Since slaves were investment income, planters realized it was to their advantage to keep the slaves healthy and content, by providing them with the minimum requirements of adequate housing, proper food and clothing. Some mid-Century statistics for rate of growth of the slave population indicates that blacks' rate of population growth exceeded that of whites in the St. Mary Parish (Broussard, 1955).

The largest plantation owner in the area was John Newton Pharr (Conrad, 1979; Eisterhold, 1960). He was one of five people in the area owning over 100 slaves (Conrad, 1979; Eisterhold, 1960). John Pharr settled near Centerville, Louisiana, in the 1840's. He worked as an independent ax-man before he began selling timber to area mills. He eventually accumulated enough money to hire his own crew. He owned and operated four plantations: Orange Grove, Avoca Island, Glenwild, and Fairview

Rate of Population Growth, St. Mary Parish

1850	Numbers	Percentage
Whites	3,423	24.09
Free Colored	424	3.10
Slaves	9,850	71.91
	13,697	100.00
1860	Numbers	Percentage
Whites	3,508	20.86
Free Colored	251	1.49
Slaves	13,057	77.65
	16,816	100.00

(Broussard, 1955).

(Fortier, 1909).

For fifty-three years John Pharr was actively identified with the planting and manufacturing industry in both St. Mary and Iberia Parishes. He was born in Mecklenburg County, North Carolina, March 19, 1829, and was of Scottish descent (Fortier, 1909). His Presbyterian family quickly became a conspicuous part of the histories of North and South Carolina.

At the age of twenty-one he left his parents for Louisiana, there to become the master of his own fate and future. By the time of his death in 1903 Pharr would own the huge Orange Grove plantation and the equally large Avoca Island, Glenwild and Fairview plantations in St. Mary and New Iberia Parishes (Fortier, 1909).

Mr. Pharr also bought steamboats and built a small steam mill (Broussard, 1955). About the time people began converting to steam from water as a means of locomotion there appeared a change in the process of sugar production (Bathe, 1935). Central sugar-processing factories were being established, creating large systems as opposed to the small plantation sugar systems. Smaller growers now sold their cane to these large central plantations (Conrad, 1979). Instead of the slow method of handling with mules and carts through a sometime tedious transportation route, new narrow-gauge railroads were introduced to haul the cane from field to factory (Conrad,

1979). With this invention, Centerville became a major rail thoroughfare because it was situated in the middle of the Louisiana sugar-producing country. Among the largest factories of this new sugar plantation system was Orange Grove, located on the plantation owned by John Pharr (Conrad, 1979). The plantation area was just north of the heart of Centerville. This would be the birthplace of William Joseph Seymour (Nelson, 1981; Nickel, 1979; Tinney, 1978).

The end of the Civil War brought about the financial ruin of many Southern plantations. John Pharr continued to prosper, however. He continued to employ his slaves after emancipation to cut and sell timber to area planters and mills in the vicinity of the Bayou Teche, while also tending sugar cane (Eisterhold, 1960). With his keen foresight, over the course of a few years he had become a wealthy man. Pharr also took a deep interest in political life. His family, who had been Whigs before the Civil War (Fortier, 1909; Chambers, 1925); Eisterhold, 1960), became Democrats after the War. It was the Negro issue and the hated Reconstruction policy of the Republican administration that led him to change parties. In 1896, he ran as the Democratic candidate for governor (Fortier, 1909; Chambers, 1925). He won the election, according to the *New Orleans Time Democratic* newspaper, although he was denied the position, because of political maneuvering (Eisterhold, 1960; Chambers, 1925; Fortier, 1909). He carried twenty of the twenty-five white parishes, but he did not receive a majority in any parish predominantly populated by blacks (Fortier, 1909).

John Pharr married Henrietta Clara Andrus on August 11, 1868. It was the year after William's father, Simon, had married his mother Phillis in Centerville on the Orange Grove plantation owned by Mr. Pharr (Chambers, 1925; Fortier, 1909). Mrs. Pharr was of Spanish and French lineage (Chambers, 1925; Fortier, 1909). Her family had come from Spain and settled in Louisiana before the French sold the territory to the United States (Nelson, 1981; Nickel, 1979; Tinney, 1978). When Pharr married Henrietta, he added to his wealth because of her inherited land holdings. Her grandfather had owned a large cotton plantation in

Opelousas, Louisiana. Her brothers both died young, leaving the wealth to her and her mother. After the Civil War they were left in somewhat dire straits, so they moved to Iberia where she met Mr. Pharr who had industries in both St. Mary and Iberia Parishes. She brought with her an ex-slave servant named Phillis Seliba. It is this black woman with a Spanish surname who would become the mother of William Joseph Seymour.[9]

The Pharrs were Presbyterians, but Mrs. Pharr, who had converted from Catholicism (Fortier, 1909) to Methodism, seemed to be religiously supportive of all eight churches in the parish (Broussard, 1955). It was said that together Mr. and Mrs. Pharr worked for the advancement of Christianity and education (Fortier, 1909).

Seymour's Parents: A Family History

William Joseph Seymour was born on May 2, 1870. William was the first son of Simon Simon, a mulatto of Iberia Parish, in the city of St. Martinville, and a black woman named Phillis Seliba. Both had been former slaves. Phillis lived in Centerville and was employed by the John Newton Pharr family. When William Seymour filled out his marriage license in Los Angeles, California in 1908, he listed Phillis Salabarr and Simon Seymour as his parents (Fortier, 1909; Chambers, 1925) and Centerville, Louisiana, as the place of his birth. The spelling of his mother's name had changed from what appeared on the original marriage license of 1867 and the St. Mary Parish Census of 1880.[10] In both of these documents Phillis was spelled Phillis and Salabarr was rendered Seliba.[11]

Simon Simon, as his father was known until 1880, married Phillis on July 24, 1867. To this union would be born four children. William would be the first, followed by Simon Jr., Amos, and a female who is unnamed on the 1880 birth records.[12] When Simon married Phillis Seliba, in July of 1867, according to the original marriage license, he had to obtain special permission:

> Known whereas, the above bound Simon Simon has
> this day obtained from the Honorable, District Court, of

the Parish of St. Mary, a Special License to make contract a marriage with Phillis Seliba of said parish and state.

Wherefore, if no legal impediment exists against such marriage, and mean this obligation to be null and void; otherwise to remain in full force and virtue in law" (State of Louisiana, 1867).[13]

The document was signed by Simon Simon and a Mr. Washington Mitchell. It is assumed that Mr. Mitchell was white. There are many records from this period in which whites acted as witnesses for Negroes. This held true for social events such as weddings and baptisms, as well as for business enterprises and was a remnant of slavery in which slaves were considered property with no personal legal standing (Baker, 1982; Blockson, 1977; Kramer, 1982). Even into Reconstruction and beyond these types of protocols persisted.

It could be that Simon and Phillis had already married without the supervision of proper authorities and the signature of Mr. Mitchell is to simply legalize an already created arrangement.

According to the Civil Code of Louisiana as it read in 1855,

All persons authorized to celebrate marriages were required to obtain a written permit from the person empowered to grant it in the parish in which the marriage was celebrated.

During Reconstruction in Louisiana, the legislature enacted a statute providing that all private and religious marriages contracted in the State prior to an 1865 Act, especially those which were null and void because of legal provisions forbidding the intermarriage of white and colored persons, could be legalized within a two-year period by an authentic act before a notary public. Given the fact that Simon was a mulatto and Phillis a black woman, there might have been some complications. The benefits of this 1865 law also applied to parties living together as man and wife prior to the enactment of the Act, provided they wanted to contract a legal marriage.

Simon Simon, like so many ex-African slaves, had received his name either from his master, as appears to be the case here, or directly from the Bible, which also seems possible (Blockson, 1977; Genovese, 1974; Gutman, 1976; Pinder, 1997). He would retain this double Simon Simon name until sometime after emancipation. After the Emancipation of 1865 all slaves were freed by ratification of the 13th Amendment. Many former slaves, not only to distance themselves from their former slave lives, but also to start afresh, contrived new identities by changing of their name. Brenda Square, an archivist at the Amistad Research Center at Tulane University, New Orleans, relates the all too common experience of Freed Blackmen who for various reasons changed their names after emancipation.

Brenda tells of a father whose son got into trouble with the white law in Baton Rouge during the turbulent times of the post-Reconstruction era. His father's suggestion to him was to leave and later, "...I will send you a name." At a family reunion later this explanation was given for the two different family names of the same family.[14]

By 1880 Simon Simon had acquired for himself and his family the name of Simon Seymour. Simon would have been well aware of the importance and prominence of the Seymour surname. A former governor of New York who had nominated by the Democratic party to be president of the United States was named Seymour. He would run against and lose to the Civil War hero Ulysses S. Grant, also of New York. In Louisiana both on the Pharr plantation, home of William's mother, and in St. Martinville, home of his father, the Seymour name had become not only popular, but was on the lips of all white Louisianans. For reactionary Whites, the election of a Democrat would mean an end to the Radical Republicans and "Negro control" of Louisiana politics. Unfortunately, for them, with the loss of the Democratic candidate Horatio Seymour in the 1868 presidential election, Louisiana would be plunged into a period of racial disorder under the Republican-run Reconstruction.[15]

William J. Seymour's Early Life

Simon called his first son simply William, but by 1880 he would also be called William J. Seymour after the famous

Louisianan William Johnson Seymour. William Johnson Seymour had been a Confederate soldier hero who was a member of the famed Louisiana Tigers (Jones, 1991). He had fought at the battle of Fort Jackson in 1862, where the Confederates fought to prevent New Orleans from being taken. He was also a newspaper editor and in his later years headed the *Daily-Democratic* newspaper in New Orleans (Jones, 1991).

William Johnson Seymour, who at first went by William J. Seymour, was part of the Connecticut Seymour family and was a distant relative of 1868 presidential candidate Horatio Seymour. Exactly when William J. became William Joseph is unclear. Joseph is first officially used in 1908 when it appeared on William's marriage license to Jennie Moore in Los Angeles (Nelson, 1981).

The Simon Seymours lived between St. Mary Parish and the parish of Iberia, home of Simon until his untimely death in 1884 (Conrad, 1979). Simon worked untiringly during the Republican Administration of Governor William Pitt Kellogg, having been appointed a municipal judge and constable in Iberia Parish during Reconstruction (Bergerie, 1942).

Simon was a figure who which is depicted in African-American Christianity as a looming figure with pronounced African or "Negroid" features lifting the heavy cross of Christ. The theme of the African Simon helping Christ on the way to Calvary was popular as a religious rallying point with blacks, so the name was given to slaves frequently by their parents.

Marcus Garvey in a 1921 speech makes clear the importance of the Simon character and the Simon name:

Oh Jesus, the redeemer, when white men scorned you, when white men spurned you, when white men spat upon you, when white men pierced your side....it was a black man in the person of Simon the Cyrenian who took the cross and bore it to heights of Calvary. As he bore it in your Calvary, so now, when we are climbing our Calvary and the burden being heavy -- Jesus we ask you to help us on the journey up the heights (Pinder, 1997, p. 231).

Little William grew as did his share of plantation toil. In those days every child helped the family to survive. William, a strong and husky youth, soon shouldered a grown man's burden. He received little or no real formal schooling but in the best American frontier tradition managed to educate himself and learn to read and write (Nelson, 1981; Shumway, 1914).

Seymour drank deeply from a "wellspring of spirituality." He developed a strong and abiding love for the Negro Spirituals sung in the cane fields during the heat of the day (DuBois, 1903; Fischer, 1953; Johnson, 1956; Lovell, 1939; Nelson, 1981). He had come from a broad-based religious heritage. His mother was the product of Catholicism, Methodism and Presbyterianism (Broussard, 1955; Fortier, 1909). His father was, of course, French Cajun Roman Catholic (Perrin, 1891). Thus, early on, he came to appreciate the black faith tradition (Henry, 1970; Marshall, 1970; Raboteau, 1995; Sernett, 1975).

Under the patronage of Mr. Pharr, William J. grew to manhood, getting a first-hand account of the harsh Louisiana brand of Jim Crow in a society racked with the social injuries and divisions left behind by slavery. His young life was full of several visions of an acute spiritual nature (Nelson, 1981; Nickel, 1979; Tinney, 1978). He was a sensitive and spirit-minded youth whose spiritual awareness was obvious even in his youth. He grew up looking for the apocalyptic glorious coming again of the Lord Jesus Christ (Shumway, 1914). It was these divine epiphanies that would guide him throughout his life, allowing for a special stability and confidence.

School Days

On the Louisiana plantation where She grew up, Sarah Benjamin, recalled, "...the white folks had beat all the learning out of me" (Litwack, 1972, p. 53). But some blacks through their own initiative acquired rudimentary education, sometimes at clandestine schools, others in the public schools tolerated in a few communities. Like many young blacks, whenever the opportunity presented itself, William tried to take advantage of those moments.

The curiosity of education consistently beckoned William. As for Booker T. Washington, for William the mysteries of reading and writing acted like sirens in the night. Once he learned the danger of reading, said Booker T. Washington, he was even more anxious to acquire the skill (Washington, 1909). Because after emancipation, employers and landlords, storekeepers, and others took every opportunity to exploit black illiteracy, it became of paramount importance to young William to be able to read and write. He learned quickly how critical education was. At no time was it more important than when "settling up" time came for sharecroppers, or the signing of labor contracts for freedmen that involved rates of wages and interest. Learning how to read, write and 'cipher' were deemed essential the moment emancipation was announced. It was reason enough for one Louisiana neighbor of William's to send his children to school even if their absence from the fields deprived the family of additional earnings (Litwack, 1998). "Education only hurts a fool," he decided (Litwack, 1998, p. 54). He wanted them to know enough about "figgering and keeping accounts so nobody could take advantage of them" (Litwack, 1998, p.54).

William's family understood that the ability of reading and writing not only provided some protection from white exploitation but also improved the prospects for different kinds of work possibilities. From the moment that schools were available after the War and during Reconstruction, blacks flocked to them in impressive numbers (Litwack, 1998). Like most children, William received only the amount of education that was available to him. According to Sam Gadsen, born in 1882, fifth grade was "the top grade for us in those years" (Gadsen, 1974). West T. Jones, a more closely related contemporary of William's, born in 1872, managed to complete the sixth grade (Brown, 1981). Anything beyond the eighth grade was a rarity as well as a luxury during William's time. Few high schools were available for blacks, and what little education they did receive hardly prepared them for the more advanced grades (Litwack, 1998).

It was felt by whites and frustrated blacks alike that education beyond the rudimentary level only invited higher feelings of aspiration and greater ambitions than could be fulfilled. Benjamin Mays, wanted to continue his education, but was told by his father that there were only two "honest occupations" for black men: preaching and farming (Johnson, 1941, p. 356). As for the ministry, he deemed an education really unnecessary. "God 'called' men to preach; and when he called them, he would tell them what to say!" (Johnson, 1941, p. 356).

After emancipation the Freedmen's Bureau and various northern missionary societies attempted to meet the educational needs of young blacks like William. In many cases the enthusiasm for learning led blacks to take the initiative independent of white authority for their own education. William could have attended classes anywhere -- in an abandoned cabin converted into an instant schoolhouse, mule stables, plantation cotton house, warehouse, storeroom, discarded white school, buildings owned by black fraternal orders, and, most commonly in black churches. Mary Jane Wilson, an 1874 graduate of Hampton Institute, proudly said, "...I had my graduation exercises in the Emmanuel A.M.E. Church..." (Morton, 1922, p. 13). The schools that William attended were no different from other rural Southern schools for blacks. They all looked very much alike. The conditions were makeshift, primitive, unpainted one-room board structures, with shaky floors and cracks in the walls and roof: the pot-bellied, wood-burning stove stood in the center of the room. The students sat on crude hard, backless benches made of split logs with the teachers sitting at the front of the class. Leon Litwack reports that sometimes the teacher's desk was fenced in with a railing (Litwack, 1998). School supplies had to be furnished by the teacher. They were found many times by scouting through dumps and trash piles of the neighborhood (Beam, 1967; Davis, 1969; Johnson, 1933; Mays, 1971; Proctor, 1925). Mary McLeod Bethune tells the story of how she used charred splinters for pencils and mashed elderberries for ink (Harlon, 1972).

William's school term would have varied with labor demands as well as weather conditions and even social conditions. Usually children only came to school after crop picking time. This was usually in November, but could be as late as January. They would leave in early Spring just in time to prepare the field for new crops. If school consisted of a full five months, then they were doing well. While crops were being harvested, it was the younger children who went to school. On rainy days the older children might come, thus swelling the numbers.

What William learned in school was expected to focus primarily on morality, productive labor, and a life of continued social accommodation. He was lectured about self-improvement and taught the biographies of self-made men. There was the lesson of patriotism and democracy, preached with American fervency. He was taught that success came through hard work, soberness, and honesty and to those who adopted the ethics of diligence, perseverance, punctuality, faithfulness, and respect for authority. He was taught the gospel of the superiority of Anglo Saxon institutions. The history of black people would have been seldom, if at all, mentioned. And when it was mentioned it was talked about in terms of submission gladly endured (Litwack, 1998).

Being a son of the defeated South, and the first generation of freedom, William was taught everything with a distinctive Southern bias. The historian Leon Litwack mentions a northerner visiting a small southern black school during Reconstruction who was taken aback to hear some five hundred black children sing,

> In Dixie Land
> I take my stand
> To live and die in Dixie

(Litwack, 1998).

Not all black educational programs fared well. William's school, like all others, would have been under the constant threat of being closed by angry whites. The sight of black children carrying books often had the same effect on whites as the sight of armed blacks (Litwack, 1998). Many black children hid their books until they reached school, fearing harassment if whites saw them going to school. In 1868 the diary of Nimrod Porter records that, "the Ku Klux Klan ordered the school mistress to stop her school. She done so and told the children to go home, so the school is broken up" (Litwack, 1972, pp. 487-88).

In Louisiana equality, even in the post-emancipation period, seemed to be elusive. By the end of Reconstruction the issue in Louisiana was settled. An 1874 New Orleans newspaper declared, "The only condition under which the two races can co-exist peacefully is when the superior race shall control and the inferior race shall obey." This editorial comment came in response to white mobs that were conducting raids around the state expelling Negroes from city schools. It was in such a horrendous social climate that young William turned increasingly to the church for help, guidance, and direction.

A Time Worse Than Slavery

William Seymour grew up in the midst of the violent racial aftermath of the Civil War. Through legislation and judicial decision, many hoped that the reconstruction of the South following the war would be a time of healing for the Union. Instead it turned out to be a time of awesome suffering, charged with elements of fear, jealousy, proscription, hatred, continued racism, and fanaticism (Woodward, 1966). The period between Reconstruction and the turn of the Century created a system of "consistent, thorough and legally sanctioned segregation" (Woodward, 1966, p. 25). The period from 1865 to 1890 for the South as a whole was one of violent flux and change, during which the Negro came to recognize and to comply with a code stronger than the law, a code which marked the completion of the transition from slavery to caste as a method of social control. It was so cruel a system that it is generally said that by 1890, even before the advent of Jim Crow legislation, the Negro was "in his place" (Wharton, 1947, pp. 274-76).

There were areas though, especially in Louisiana up until 1898, where Negroes had exercised considerable political influence by voting, holding state and local offices, receiving federal and state patronage, and participating in party conventions and councils. In these areas the Negro did possess greater civil rights, though limited, during this period. He served on juries and often exercised his rights of assembly, speech and press freely and sometimes to considerable effect. While his social movements did encounter strong restraints, he was, in some areas of Louisiana, subject to fewer restrictions and less discrimination than before the enactment of Jim Crow legislation. It was during this time that William's father, Simon, served as a municipal judge and constable in Iberia Parish (Bergerie, 1962).

The degree to which the Negro could exercise his political, social and civil rights depended upon a wide range of circumstances, as did the degree of discrimination to which he was subjected (Logan, 1964; Wharton, 1947; Woodward, 1966; Wynes, 1961). Perhaps the most striking aspect of race relations in Louisiana from 1877 to 1898 was the absence of a consistent system. While in general Negroes in Louisiana occupied a socially and economically depressed position, a marked exception to the generally depressed condition of Louisiana Negroes was the status of the descendants of the "free people of color:" "gens de couleur libres" as they had originally been called by the French (McTigue, 1975). These Negroes had for years enjoyed freedom. They differed from their emancipated Negro counterparts in that they had been free even before reconstruction. They had for years lived free in Louisiana, creating for themselves wealth, education, and a prominent social and political status. Many had even been educated in France. They were generally respected by whites.

While William Seymour's father was definitely not of the "gens de couleur libres" class, he was still probably highly respected by whites living in his parish, because it is these whites who appointed him a municipal judge and constable during the Reconstruction period (Bergerie, 1962). But it is still the overall theme of the failings of reconstruction, as displayed in corruption by whites who used the Negroes as pawns and puppets, which rendered as tragedy Simon Seymour's short tenure as judge.

The Life and Death of Simon Seymour

It is under these perverse Reconstruction conditions in 1884 that Simon Seymour, William's father, was murdered. He was 43 years old. He had been born in 1841 in St. Mary Parish and was the property of Edward J. Simon (Chambers, 1925; Nelson, 1981; Nickel, 1979; Perrin, 1891). Edward J. Simon was born in 1827, in St. Mary Parish, but for the greater part of his life resided in St. Martinville, where he became a distinguished lawyer and served as judge (Chambers, 1925). He served on the Supreme Court of the State of Louisiana from January 1, 1840-March 19, 1846 (Dart, 1933). His son, James, and grandson, James D., both served distinguished careers as jurists in Louisiana. It was because of this family's extraordinary service as lawyers and judges that Simon, their former slave, was also appointed a municipal judge and parish constable during Reconstruction (Bergerie, 1962). He became a Republican as did most newly emancipated Negro slaves. This party affiliation would contribute to his death in 1884 (Bergerie, 1962).

The Louisiana Republican party, according to author Gerard Conrad, was split into at least two factions (Conrad, 1979). One faction of the party used the newly enfranchised Negroes for their own political ends. This faction became known as the "Black Republicans" (Conrad, 1979). The other faction of the State Republican party was called the "Lily Whites," because they refused to use the Negro vote altogether (Conrad, 1979).

The warring Reconstruction Republican party in Louisiana would lose its short-lived political control of the state with the 1876 election of Francis T. Nicholls, the first Democratic governor of Louisiana since the Civil War. Thus ended the Republican regime in the State House. However, it was not until 1884 that the Republicans lost power in Iberia Parish. This was the Parish where the Simon Seymours lived.

The animosity between the factions of the Republican party and between the Republican and Democratic parties in Iberia Parish reached a climax in April of 1884. The election of local and Parish officials caused disruptions which turned Iberia Parish into a virtual battleground. The switching back and forth of Democrats to Republicans and Republicans to Democrats, not to mention the intra-party tensions, helped to heighten an already deteriorating situation. Both parties organized paramilitary groups for protection (Conrad, 1981).

During September and October, 1884, shots had been fired at Democratic candidates in the Parish (Conrad, 1981). Although all had escaped injury, the incident increased tensions among all factions.

On November 1, 1884, just before the Congressional and presidential elections, a Republican rally was held in the Iberian Parish town of Loreauville on behalf of Republican candidates for Congress. Among the small number of whites who attended were about three hundred blacks (Conrad, 1981). Judge Simon Seymour (Bergerie, 1962; Conrad, 1981) was a part of this rally.

The Battle of Loreauville

According to one account, the speech makers were confronted by a group of Loreauville citizens who asked about what they considered to be verbal abuse of the Democratic candidate for judge of Iberia Parish, Edward J. Gay (Conrad, 1981). During this face-to-face encounter, a shot rang out and there was a "general resort to firearms" (Conrad, 1981). The crowd panicked. There was a mass trampling as people tried to flee the flying bullets. When the shooting ended an undisclosed number of blacks were dead. Among the dead was Simon Seymour (Conrad, 1981).

The "Battle of Loreauville", as the incident was dubbed by the New Orleans *Daily Picayne* and the New Orleans *Times Democrat*, ended Republican rule in Iberia Parish.[16] Three days later the Democratic Congress easily won all of the Parish elections. Local Republican leaders who had attended the rally were arrested and held for a time in guarded cells (Conrad, 1981).[17]

With the death of Simon, Phillis took her children, William, Simon, Amos, and her infant daughter, and they moved back to Centerville, St. Mary's Parish, Louisiana. For the next ten years William would grow up working and learning bits and pieces of the lumber and sawmill industry while on the Pharr plantation. Later he would use his carpentry skills by building the first pews for the Los Angeles Azusa Street Mission, as well as the pulpit, out of wooden shoe boxes (Ewart, 1947; Nelson, 1981).

What after all, am I? Am I an American or am I a Negro? Can I be both? Or is it my duty to cease to be a Negro as soon as possible and be an American? If I strive as a Negro, am I not perpetuating the very cleft that threatens and separates black and white America? Is not my only possible practical aim the subduction of all that is Negro in me to the American? Does my black blood place upon me any more obligation to assert my nationality than German, or Irish or Italian blood would?

W. E. B. DuBois (1897)

CHAPTER 3
THE MIDDLE YEARS

William came of age during the time when Louisiana was considered part of the New South, the time after Emancipation and during Reconstruction. His life exemplifies all the contradictions of black life and coming of age in the New South. These include the initial hopes and aspirations, the often heightened expectations, as well as the frustrations, the terrors, the tensions, the betrayals, and the necessary accommodations (Litwack, 1998). Although he was among the first blacks born in freedom, coming to maturity in the late nineteenth and early twentieth century, he was a part of a society in which the extraordinary power of white people was wielded over black people in every phase of their daily lives. Ex-slave Ardie Clerk Halyard in her memoirs stated succinctly for all blacks, "The only thing that you would be thinking of, ...was, ... that they were the ones that had everything" (Hill, 1991, p. 23).

Because the racial boundaries and modes of behavior and social interaction had been defined by centuries of strictly enforced custom and thoughts, every black child, little William included, would have come to accept the terribly unfair social system in which they lived. William would have learned like all black children to curb his ambitions, limit his options, and carefully consider every gesture, word, and movement while in the presence of whites. It was part of the art of survival. Any deviation from what whites expected of you could lead to immediate and often violent reprisal (Litwack, 1998). Benjamin Mays, author, historian and educator, recalling his childhood said, "If a black boy wanted to live a halfway normal life and die a natural death he had to learn early the art of how to get along with white folks" (Mays, 1971, p. 22).

William shared a common training with generations of black youth. It was based on personal early racial experiences. The "initial revelation," as I choose to call it, consisted of the moment that the meaning and force of race became the defining issue for the rest of your life. It might be triggered by a physical altercation or oral abuse, or something as simple as an incriminating glance or a hostile exchange of words. But for most young black children the encounter, though universal, was nonetheless shocking, and more times than not traumatic, and almost always permanent. By the time William's father was murdered at the hands of white men in 1884 (Conrad, 1979), the sore had healed, producing a highly visible keloid-like scar of remembrance. One contemporary of William's, Robert Russa Morton, summed it up by saying, "We always remembered dare waz a diffrunce. We didn't forget we waz black" (Perdue, 1976, 1939, p. 73).

The humiliation is what remained so vividly in the minds of blacks as it came with all haste without provocation and usually with no explanation. Mary Church, another Seymour contemporary, remembers being forcibly removed from a railroad coach as a little girl. After inquiring of other passengers, the conductor loudly asked, "Whose little Nigger is this?" (Terrell, 1940, pp. 15-16). Mary Church's embarrassment and humiliation lived forever. Louis Armstrong recalls in 1905 when a friend of his mother's dragged him to the rear of the Tulane Avenue Trolley in New Orleans because he had sat himself in front of the sign that read, "For Colored Passengers Only" (Armstrong, 1954). He was supposed to have been behind the sign.

The indignities perpetuated on black youths were meant to impress on this new post-emancipation generation the solidity of racial lines and the unchallengeable authority and superiority of the dominant race (Litwack, 1998). But while the harassment of racial humiliation forced them to recognize their limitations, it also awakened in many a new sense of black identity, a capacity for rage, and in some cases the rationale and the willingness to cross white lines -- all of which, explains Leon Litwack, needed to be contained if they were to survive (Litwack, 1998). William, like many other blacks looking for ways of coping psychologically with such a harsh life, turned toward God. He early on, like Benjamin Mays, had decided, "...that God would mete out the punishment that Negroes were powerless to inflict (Litwack, 1998, Mays, 1991; Robinson, 1950).

Young blacks went through their rites of passage in a number of ways. But the specter and threat of physical violence[18] -- "The white death," as Leon Litwack calls it -- loomed over nearly every encounter (Litwack, 1998). Even if they themselves were not the victims, the violence fell on family, friends and neighbors. Every black person knew some black person who had fallen prey to the "white death." It was always imposed to remind blacks of their place, punishing any signs of independence, impertinence and impudence, always making sure that the diseases of being "sassy" or "uppity" didn't spread among the general black population. Young William, like most young blacks, would have come to understand both the frequency and the random nature of these violent racial attacks. They knew and accepted the fact that they were designed not only to punish, but also to send a message to the entire black community. Like all black youth, William's memory included beatings, lynchings, burnings, and a host of despicable acts the memory of which could not be easily erased (King, 1980; Murray, 1956; Wright, 1945). In the town in which William grew up as a child, New Iberia, Louisiana, Audley Moore, a parish neighbor, recalls the horrible sight of her first lynching. It happened before the turn of the Century while William was still living there.

> I remember Grandma allowing us to look through the shutter and be careful not to open it too much, so they wouldn't see us. The victim was being drawn by a wagon. He was tied and his head was bumping up and down on the clay, the hard, crusty road...and the mean hollering behind; white men, like wolves, were behind this man. Well, you know that's a terrible thing for a child to see, and you grow up that way... (Wright, 1965, pp. 69-70).

There seemed to be no legal redress. The difference between "justice" and lawlessness was not apparent. Black youth early on learned to fear the law. The image of the policeman was always tantamount to the enemy. Albon Holsey, another contemporary of William J. Seymour, stated that he lived in "mortal fear" of the police, "for they were arch-tormenters and persecutors of Negroes...I ran from policemen so often when I was a boy that even now [1929], though I am past forty, if one walks upon me unexpectedly my first impulse is to take to my heels (Murray, 1929).

Black boys like William were always reminded that white men with hounds and guns were not always overly particular about whom they caught in their manhunts. The object was to bring back a black body, not necessarily the guilty party (Hudson, 1972). The subject of the police was common talk among black boys growing up in William's day. The stories all revolved around scenes of chases, harassment, clubbing, illegal arrests, and forced confessions (Litwack, 1998).

Black youths of William's day knew well the patterns of racial etiquette. They knew they were rigidly separated from whites; they were forbidden to enter parks, libraries, restaurants and even some churches. They were fully conscious of all the social mores that sanctioned the ritualized subservience which became a part of their lives. Like Albon Holsey, William and other young blacks of his generation sensed that the odds were stacked against them, no matter what they did.

At fifteen, I was fully conscious of the racial difference, and while I was sullen and resentful in my soul, I was beaten and knew it. I knew then that I could never aspire to be President of the United States, nor Governor of my state, nor Mayor of my city; I knew that the front doors of white homes in my town were not for me to enter, except as a servant, I know that I could only sit in the peanut gallery at our theater, and could only ride on the back of the electric car and in the Jim Crow car on the train. I had bumped into the color line and knew that so far as white

The lynching of John Richards, Goldsboro, North Carolina. This picture appears in *Without Sanctuary*, Twin Palms Publishers, Santa Fe, New Mexico.

people were concerned, I was just another Nigger (Holsey, 1929, p. 423).

Race consciousness came early for young William. By adolescence he had already experienced in a variety of ways the racial mores and etiquette of what was supposed to be the New South (Litwack, 1998). By age ten, he had already run the entire gauntlet of racial baptisms (Holsey, 1929). But what must have created the most chagrin for William and millions of black youth like him were the feelings of helplessness, frustration, humiliation, and the inability to do anything about their predicament.

As William grew older, reaching adolescence, he, like other children, began to compare his situation with those of the white children around them. He asked the same questions that had been asked for generations. Could things be different? What could a black youth look forward to becoming? Like Rosa Parks, the mother of the twentieth-century Civil Rights Movement, he asked, "If we are free people...why we had to be deprived of the better things..." (Hill, 1991, p. 23). Like Richard Wright, premier black American author, he asked, "What was it that made the hate of whites for blacks so steady, seemingly so woven into the texture of things?" (Hill, 1991, p. 23). But with no satisfactory answers given and trying to make sense of the world around him, young William like so many black youths before him learned to control his instincts and ambitions. He learned ways to adapt and accommodate. He acquired the proper demeanor and he knew the proper responses. As Benjamin Mays, great black American Civil Rights leader said, "it was always the Negroes' responsibility to find ways and means to get along with white people" (Mays, 1971, p. 26). He had acquired, like generations of black men and women before him, the necessary skills of obsequiousness, duplicity, humility, flattery, and evasion (Litwack, 1998). He mastered the ability to anticipate the moods, whims, and expectations of white families, the knowledge of how to massage their egos and feed their self-esteem, and the sense of when to feign stupidity, even to "act the Nigger" (Litwack, 1998). All of this posturing and manipulation allowed little William the "luxury" of surviving into manhood.

The lynching of Laura Nelson, Okemah, Oklahoma. Picture appears in *Without Sanctuary*, Twin Palms Publishers, Santa Fe, New Mexico.

The trauma of childhood shaped the life, personality and character of William Joseph Seymour. For William, growing up in the late nineteenth century, the residue of enslavement and the betrayal of emancipation served not only to reinforce the bitterness he felt over his condition, but as with so many other black young men before him, it propelled him to do something -- anything. When, after the brutal death of his father in 1884 (Conrad, 1979), and the feelings of "I can't take this any longer" loomed larger in his psyche than the ability to tolerate continuing acts of accommodations, acquiescence and obsequience, he left. In 1895, with no possessions, he hopped on a freight train in Centerville, the railroad capital of sugar cane country, and headed North (MacRobert, 1988; Nelson, 1981).

An early image of W. J. Seymour as seen in *The Life and Ministry of William J. Seymour* **by Larry Martin.**

I will find a way or make one.
                        Motto of Yale's Class of 1863

CHAPTER 4
THE EXODUS
William Leaves the South

William, who was 25 in 1895, had experienced enough of the brutal politics of Louisiana. He had seen his father murdered in a political war in 1884 (Bergerie, 1962). Now, on the plantation home of his birth, political trouble was again stirring as his boss, Mr. Pharr, ran for office (Pharr, 1955).

Pharr, one of Louisiana's wealthiest men by 1890, had left the Democratic Party to become a Republican. He was a gubernatorial candidate on the Republican-populist fusion ticket in 1896[19]; however, vote fraud gave the election to Murphy J. Foster (Pharr, 1955).

A desperation sounded within William. He, like other young black men, weary of the political mayhem in Louisiana which always left blacks dead, acknowledged that his life had become cheap and expendable (Litwack, 1998). He knew that to remain in the South was in itself life threatening. As another Southern boy explained, "I am sick of the South and always have been...so by God's help...I will soon be out of the South" (Litwack, 1998, p. 443).

William defended his decision against all requests to stay. He knew, like thousands of other blacks, that to stay in the South was hoping against hope. For neither character, the accumulation of property, the fostering of the church, nor the education of the schools had resulted in either respect or opportunity among the whites. No matter how hard one tried or how honest one was, if you were black, that's all that you were.

At the turn of the century, blacks left in such great numbers that it actually upset the balance of social, economic and political life in Louisiana. Richard Wright tells of his response to a white man's questions about why he was leaving for Chicago. His argument could have easily been that of William Seymour or any young black man who had spent 25 years living in the South; scared, frustrated, and just plain sick and tired.

"The North's no good for your people, boy."
"I'll try to get along, Sir."
"Don't believe all the stories you hear about the North."
"No, Sir. I don't"
"You'll come back here where your friends are."
"Well, Sir. I don't know."
"How are you going to act up there?"
"Oh, No Sir. I'll act there just, just like I act here."
"Aw, No, you won't. You'll change. Niggers change when they go North."

I wanted to tell him that I was going North precisely to change, but I did not (Wright, 1938, pp. 224-25).

When William arrived in Indianapolis he found new tensions, anxieties, and betrayal. Racial differences did not always result in lynchings, Jim Crowism, peonage or disfranchisement, but he found that though this was the North, it was still America.

Life In Indianapolis

When William was 25 years old, he boarded the train whose track had been laid through Centerville when he was eight years old, and left Louisiana (Nelson, 1981; Shumway, 1914). Indianapolis, like other black destination cities, such as New York, Chicago, Cleveland, and Detroit, was relatively progressive and seemed to offer real opportunity for a young black man. It definitely was a world of difference from Louisiana. Indianapolis was the center of railroad travel in the mid-west at the time. The city proclaimed its railroad station to be the largest in the world (Nelson, 1981). It was the hub for twenty-six different lines, radiating out of Indianapolis for miles like the spokes of a great wheel (Nelson, 1981).

Upon his arrival in Indianapolis, Seymour found work as a waiter in a large downtown hotel restaurant (Nelson, 1981). The city directories of Indianapolis, 1896-1899 list him as a waiter (Shumway, 1914). It appears that waiting on tables was one of the most desirable jobs possible for black men at that time. Generally all occupations were closed to black men except for the most menial and unskilled. The desirability of being a waiter is even underscored by the fact that there was a black union for waiters in Indianapolis at a time when there were few unions for black or white workers. The union advertised frequently in Indianapolis' black newspapers (Nelson, 1981). While in Indianapolis, William took rooms located at 127-1/2 Indiana Avenue, and later, 309 Bird Street (Nelson, 1981). Both of these locations were in the central business district of downtown Indianapolis. In the city directory of 1899 he is listed at the Bird address and his occupation is given as waiter.

It is reported by Douglas Nelson that Seymour joined the Simpson Chapel Methodist Episcopal Church which was located on Missouri at Eleventh Street (Nelson, 1981). While there is no record of his membership, many blacks traveling North found refuge within Methodism. The Methodist church had a history of active outreach to slaves (Harmon, 1979; Matthews, 1963). Methodism's founder, John Wesley, had called slavery, "that execrable villainy, the scandal of religion, of England, and of human nature,..." (Harmon, 1979). Also, Williams' Louisianan roots would have made him familiar with the good works of Methodism. During Reconstruction the Northern Methodist Church became one of the main educational agencies in Louisiana, with a school near Centerville, which William may have attended as a boy (White, 1970).

Charles Shumway, in a 1914 A.B. Boston University thesis, states that while William Seymour was in Indianapolis, he was converted in a Black Methodist Episcopal Church (Shumway, 1914). It is not clear, according to Mel Robeck, Pentecostal historian, whether Shumway was referring to the African Methodist Episcopal Church, a largely African American denomination founded in 1787 by Richard Allen and other free blacks, or the Methodist Episcopal Church, North.[20] Historian Douglas Nelson suggests that the only legitimate possibility was the Methodist Episcopal Church, North, with the Simpson Chapel Methodist Episcopal Church being its Indianapolis church.

Oral tradition in Indianapolis maintains that while a member of Simpson Chapel, Seymour also aligned himself with a Holiness group called the "Evening Light Saints" and that it is actually among these people that he was converted.[21] This was confirmed by Mother Emma L. Cotton, a leader in early Los Angeles Pentecostal Movement.[22]

Simpson Chapel Methodist Episcopal Church was an interracial Methodist church (Nelson, 1981). William could have joined the strongest black Methodist church in Indianapolis, located closer to his residence on Bird Street, the Bethel African Methodist Episcopal Church on Vermont, but what he was seeking was interracial reconciliation. Bethel was associated with the all-black A.M.E. denomination started by Richard Allen at the close of the 18th Century. Allen's A.M.E. denomination had been called the "greatest Negro organization in the world" by W.E.B. DuBois (DuBois, 1968).

William Seymour had come to Indiana to rid himself of racial turmoil. Indiana had early on sought to correct past injustices done against blacks by removing all racial distinctions from its state constitution and laws. Blacks in Indiana were accorded equal protection under the law, and had the right to vote and hold office. It is obvious though that despite these constitutional guarantees there still existed discrimination and segregation based upon color. By 1900 racial attitudes in Indiana were beginning to harden. The Northern Methodist Church moved from acting out racial harmony in practice to the mere administrative formality of racial harmony in theory. With the hardening lines of racial segregation starting to appear in Indianapolis, William picked up his gear and moved in 1900 to Cincinnati.

On To Cincinnati

It is Douglas Nelson who reports that William Seymour moved to Cincinnati early in 1900 (Nelson, 1981). This move is not clearly documented, but it is generally accepted as having occurred based upon Nelson's research and oral tradition. It is assumed that William left Indianapolis in 1899, because this is the last year that his name appears in the city directory. William never mentioned Cincinnati in any known conversations, but neither does he talk about Indianapolis.

Cincinnati had been the center for the Underground Railroad. It always occupied a vital role in the fight of blacks for freedom. Perhaps Seymour here felt he could find his promised land, since Indianapolis hadn't worked out.

He looked toward Methodism again to find refuge, but as in Indianapolis, the Methodist church had joined the tide of the times and had become complacent in regard to the issue of enfranchisement for the Negro. By 1900 the prevailing mood of white America toward black people had changed. The efforts of Reconstruction to uplift black people appeared to be subsiding; new myths of scientific racial superiority were finding wide acceptance. The most respected journals of the day were beginning again to portray Black people as inferior. The Methodist Church seemed to have lost its concern over racial justice (Norwood, 1970). The publication of Charles Carroll's book, *The Negro A Beast*, appeared late in the nineteenth century, and racial attitudes of Northern whites even in the liberal Methodist church began to revert back to overt racism (Nelson, 1981). As trends within Methodism as well as other Christian churches began to become more segregated, William became more and more attached to the newly growing Holiness Movement.

While in Indianapolis, William had been attracted to the early Church of God. The Church of God sought to form the church "Of every race and color;" members referred to each other as "brothers" and "sisters." This group actually projected the goal of inter-racialism more than any other (Clear, 1977; Clemmons, 1976; Massey, 1957). The Church of God minister, William Schnell, in 1901, wrote a reply to Charles Carroll's book, *The Negro A Beast*. He attempted to prove from a Biblical, scientific, and historical perspective that the Negro was fully human (Schnell, 1901).

But it would be the Holiness ministry of the Cincinnati preacher, Martin Wells Knapp, that would change William's life forever (Jones, 1973). Knapp along with other former Methodists like Daniel S. Warner, a father of the Church of God Reformation Movement (Anderson, Indiana), and Phineas Bresee, founder of the Church of the Nazarene, belonged to an emerging late nineteenth century religious movement that was based upon Zechariah 14:7, which says, "...it shall be light." They understood this to mean that just as the early apostles had lived in the "morning light" of the Gospel era, the generation of 1880 was living at the end of time when the "evening light" was divinely ordained. They became known as the "Evening Light Saints." They had left the mainline Holiness sect for purposes of a more radical ministry. They were seeking the same Christian sanctification/perfection that John Wesley had sought when he started Methodism (Smith, 1957).

Martin Wells Knapp operated God's Bible School and Missionary Training Home. Its motto was "Back to the Bible" (Robeck, 1998). It was located on what Knapp called the "Mount of Blessings" at Ringgold, Young and Channing Streets in Cincinnati (Robeck, 1998). He also was part of the growing "Evening Light Saints" movement of the late 1890's.

Duane Windermiller, in an undated autobiography, writes about the atmosphere of the early Evening Light Movement.

> ...no music in the church, no neckties, the men greeted each other with a holy kiss (because the Bible told them to), no rings, no makeup, no hairdos, no playing cards, no bowling, no dancing, no funny papers. If this seems like a religion of no's, it is not a complete picture, for I enjoyed those years... I left this denomination -- I must say honestly -- with some deep regrets (Nelson, 1981).

The new movement reached out vigorously to black people. The Evening Light people believed that they were receiving the last spiritual outpouring just before the close of history (Clear,

Rev. D. S. Warner along with his wife. Warner is the father of the Evening Light Movement. Picture appeared in *Vital Christianity: An Historical Overview of the Church of God Movement's First Century*, June 22, 1980/Vol. 100, No. 12.

1977). Although no detailed documentation of Seymour's relationship with Knapp or Warner occurs, Seymour's Azusa Street Ministry shows many parallels with that of Knapp. Knapp described the church as follows:

> "there can be neither Jew nor Greek,... Barriers of race and color, and social position have no true place in Christ's church, *** 'High toned social clubs, claiming to be churches, but throwing stones of criticism and ostracism at saints of God because of caste or color, are among the most stupendous of satan's frauds which curse the earth today. ...Respecters and selectors of persons... What a contrast to the "Body of Christ" (Jones, 1973).

Knapp held frequent Cincinnati campaigns. He operated a downtown Cincinnati church, a training home and a summer camp in Flat Rock, Kentucky. He stressed the doctrines of divine healing, and the imminent return of the Lord Jesus. His ministry was cut short, however, when he died of typhoid fever at the age of 48 years (Nelson, 1981).

William Seymour was excited by the teaching of Knapp and grew more interested in the ministry of the Evening Light Saints. He responded especially to the racial inclusiveness of the movement and the call for sanctification. It is this meaningful interest in the Evening Light Saints, which resulted in his call to the ministry. Nelson says that Seymour first wrestled intensely, refusing to follow the divine leading (Nelson, 1981). But during a serious bout with small pox, he came to feel that God was calling him. After about three weeks of intense suffering, he accepted the call (Nelson, 1981). He survived the Cincinnati small pox epidemic of 1902, but was left, according to Nelson, with severe facial scarring and the loss of vision in his left eye. Nelson cites this as the reason William grew growing a beard. However, the issue of Seymour's blindness is disputed by Clemmons (Clemmons, 1976), but it was reported that he was blind in an article in The Los Angeles Daily Times, Wednesday, April 18, 1906, entitled, "Weird Babel of Tongues."[23]

Whether blind or not, it is clear that from 1902 on, Seymour's life was drastically changed. He entered the ministry of The Evening Light Church. He then left Cincinnati in an attempt to go back to Centerville to reunite with his brothers Simon, Jr. and Amos, his mother and his sister.

In 1902, having become a follower of Martin Wells Knapp and his doctrines of holiness, William made a spiritual commitment to become a minister of the Gospel. He received training at Knapp's bible school. Before leaving Cincinnati, however, Seymour received word that his family had left Louisiana and had moved to the Houston, Texas area (Shumway, 1914). In 1902 he left Cincinnati and headed for Texas (MacRobert, 1988), hoping to reunite with his family, whom he had not seen since leaving Centerville in 1895.

Houston, Texas 1902-1904

Around the turn of the Century, John Newton Pharr, former slave master of the Seymour family, was persuaded by a Mr. F. Blalack of San Antonio, Texas, to come and try his luck at sugar cane production in the lower Rio Grande Valley of Texas (Pharr, 1955). After a visit by Mr. Blalack to the Pharr's Centerville, Louisiana, plantation, he suggested to the Pharrs, "If you fellows can make the money you claim you are making, under the conditions existing here, I would like to show you a section in Southern Texas, where you can make more, with considerably less effort and risk" (Pharr, 1955, p. 42). The Pharrs persuaded some of their Louisiana friends and associates in the sugar industry to accompany them. By 1909 there was an entire town with the name "Pharr, Texas". The sons of John Newton Pharr had moved part of the family operation from Centerville, Louisiana to the Rio Grande Valley (Times-Picayne, New Orleans, LA., Oct. 29, 1966).

In the process of relocation, many of Pharr's Centerville workers left St. Mary Parish to come to Texas to help in the building of the new enterprise. Among those leaving Louisiana were William Seymour's brothers, Simon Jr. and Amos, now in their twenties, along with their mother, Phillis, and their young sister. They, like other "exodusters," were looking for a better life and better opportunities. Texas had become a desirable destination for Louisiana's black emigres. In Texas, black Louisianans felt safe and free, hoping that the broad spaces would provide ample room for growth. Though many Louisiana plantation owners tried to persuade emancipated blacks not to abandon Louisiana, nothing could halt the westward migration (Conrad, 1980).

When William got word that his family had moved to the Houston area, he left Cincinnati and headed immediately for Texas. While it is not clear if he ever found them or not, it is clear that by 1903 he was living in Houston, Texas (Shumway, 1914). William never mentioned his family and they never show up in the history of William Joseph Seymour's life.

While William did go to Texas to search for his family, there is no record of him going to the Pharr, Texas, area which is probably where his family was. He was probably unaware of Pharr, Texas, as Pharr didn't really begin to flourish as a town until around 1908 (Pharr, 1955; Times-Picayne, New Orleans, Oct. 29, 1966).

The Lost Seymours

While there is no record of William Seymour's ever reuniting with his family, there remains the possibility that William's family became part of the great reconstruction Black migration movement (Redkey, 1969). Just eleven miles south of Pharr, Texas, was the Texas-Mexican border. One of the dreams of the Pharr community was to establish a link between its community and Mexico. The residents of Pharr came to understand that its economic growth depended on trade with the Mexican nation and its citizens. To the south of Pharr was the Mexican town of Reynosa.

Mexico was one of the areas to which Blacks would migrate during reconstruction, in search of real freedom and to escape from the harshness of Jim Crow politics. The Black migration movement, although always a part of the black community's social history, was fragmented, sporadic, and divided (Redkey, 1969). During the dark days following the Civil War the movement was able to make its most dramatic strides. During this time the United States wrestled with the question, "What should we do with the Negro?" The African-American increasingly looked to Africa, Mexico, Central America, Haiti; or the territory of Oklahoma for safe haven (Redkey, 1969; Barboza, 1993; Lewis, 1993).

Even Abraham Lincoln had favored schemes to settle freed slaves in areas outside of the United States (Redkey, 1969; Wilmore, 1973; Lewis, 1993).

By 1890, with the failure of cotton and sugar cane, the number of requests for emigration rose drastically at the offices of the American Colonization Society (Redkey, 1969). The changes in the market prices had caused tremendous economic stress.

Falling prices caused farmers to raise more crops. The influx on the market caused prices to drop. The South was devastated. Rather than fight the political and economic hardships a great number of blacks attempted emigration.

In a letter to the American Colonization Society,[24] one man said: "The new constitution and oppressive laws is the reason we want to emigrate" (Redkey, 1969).

Another request stated:

> ...we are as people oppressed and disfranchised we are still working hard and our rights taken from us times are hard and getting harder every year we as people believe that Africa is the place, but to get from under bondage our thinking is of Oklahoma. As this is our nearest place of safety. ... (Redkey, 1969).

One man said: "The Negroes there isn't anything but slaves, oh my God help us to get out from here to Africa" (Redkey, 1969).

Pharr, Texas, was hard hit during this period. The only thing that saved the town was its geography. Because it was located on the Gulf of Mexico with an average annual temperature of 73 degrees, its warm winter days and soft summers made it more than able to grow all kinds of citrus fruits, vegetables, and nuts.

Eventually, the Pharr family left the area. During their departure many of the workers who had come with them began to scatter, choosing not to return to Louisiana. Many went up the road to Houston and other areas. Some, though, migrated south into Mexico. According to anthropologist Bobby Vaughn, of Stanford University, there was an already sizable Afro-Mexican population living throughout Mexico.[25]

The Afro-Mexican community dates back to 1519 when the first Africans were brought to Mexico by Spanish conquistador, Hernando Cortes. The Indians, spellbound by their dark skin, took them for gods. As late as 1772 Blacks outnumbered the Spanish in Mexico. It was not until 1810 that Spaniards were more numerous than blacks.[26]

With Reynosa being within eleven miles of Pharr, Texas, it is highly conceivable that the Seymours, like so many former Black

Picture of William J. Seymour as a young, (circa 1909), preacher. This portrait originally appeared in *The History of the Pentecostal Assemblies of the World* by Morris E. Golder, 1973.

American slaves, chose to migrate to Mexico, where they could mix in with an already existing Afro-Mexican population.

Seymour, The Evangelist

While in Houston, Seymour attached himself to the black community and to the fast emerging holiness community (Robeck, 1998). It appears that he even used Houston as a base from which he worked as a self-appointed evangelist (Nelson, 1981). He made an evangelistic trip while in Houston to Lake Charles, Louisiana (Nelson, 1981). He preached there for people who were connected with the ministerial work of Holiness preachers Charles Price Jones and Charles Harrison Mason. Both of these men would influence the spiritual development of William J. Seymour and would be a source of strength for him right up until his death in September, 1922 (Clemmons, 1981).

He would turn to Mason for advice about his marriage in 1908 (Clemmons, 1981).

In 1904 Seymour went to Jackson, Mississippi, headquarters of Charles Price Jones' ministry (Shumway, 1914). Jones had began his holiness work, after being forced out of his Baptist denomination. He, then, along with Charles Harrison Mason, had founded the Church of God in Christ in 1894 in Lexington, Mississippi (Dupree, 1996). Their emphasis on the doctrines of original sin, the Holy Ghost, Christ's atonement and Christ's second coming would become the center of Seymour's new-found faith and his personal theology (Dupree, 1996). Jones, William's mentor, would also compose many of the hymns and other music that would be used by the emerging twentieth-century Pentecostal movement (Dupree, 1996).

Seymour In Houston

Upon moving to Houston, William continued his relationship with the "Evening Light Saints," under whose influence he had come while in Cincinnati. The "Evening Light" is a term associated with the Church of God reformation movement (Sanders, 1966). The "Evening Light Saints" assumed a prophetic identity with reference to the biblical scripture of Zechariah 14:7b (KJV): "It shall come to pass, that at evening time it shall be light (Sanders, 1966).

In Houston William attended a little Holiness church that was pastored by Mrs. Lucy Farrow (Sanders, 1966; Ewart, 1975; Valdez, 1980; Tyson, 1992; Nelson, 1981; Paris, 1982; Foster, 1965; Bartleman, 1980). Mrs. Farrow was the niece of famed Black abolitionist, Frederick Douglass (Nelson, 1981; Nickel, 1979; Tinney, 1978). William who was well liked by Pastor Farrow and the congregation would eventually become the interim pastor of the small church when Pastor Farrow left in 1905. Pastor Farrow would go to Kansas to work as a "governess" in the home of Reverend Charles Fox Parham (Sanders, 1966; Nelson, 1981; Nickel, 1979; Tinney, 1978).

What an inspiration for a fatherless young man, this grandfather who always "held his head high, took no insults, made few friends. He was not a 'Negro,' he was a man!
>   The Name and Family of DuBois
>   David Levering Lewis
>   *W.E.B. DuBois: Biography of a Race* (1993)

CHAPTER 5

THE TRAILBLAZER OF PENTECOSTALISM

Charles Parham, The Pioneer

Charles Fox Parham is one of the most prolific of twentieth-century Pentecostals. No history about the movement has been, nor can be, written without an accounting of his remarkable contributions to the movement. He has been called the trailblazer (Tyson, 1992). I contend that without Parham there could have been no Seymour and, more important, no Azusa Street Revival. He has been generally known as the father of the modern Pentecostal movement (Nickel, 1979; Foster, 1965; Tyson, 1992; Paris, 1982). But there have also been those, along with me, who have questioned this assertion (Nelson, 1981; MacRobert, 1988; Tinney, 1978; Synan).

Parham, a bright young, club-footed, Bible college student in Winfield, Kansas, helped to spark the greatest revival in the twentieth century (Valdez, 1980; Tyson, 1992). While a Methodist Bible student at Southwestern College in Winfield, Kansas, Parham was instantaneously healed of his club-feet (Valdez, 1980), which had been caused by an early bout of rheumatic fever (Tyson, 1992). He felt that this was a clear sign from God of His desire for him to preach the Gospel. Although he had felt a call to ministry as early as nine years old, when he was affiliated with the Congregational Church, he had wrestled with the idea of preaching on and off until this miraculous and instantaneous healing occurred in 1891 (Tyson, 1992; Valdez, 1980). Parham had always been called the Boy Preacher, from his early days in Muscatine, Iowa, where he was born in 1873 to his days at Southwestern College.

Portrait of Rev. Charles F. Parham seated at desk. This photo appears in *The Life and Ministry of William J. Seymour* by Larry Martin.

At the age of nineteen in 1892 Charles was the youngest ordained Methodist minister in the nation (Valdez, 1980). He began his pastoral ministry in Linwood Methodist Church in Linwood, Kansas (Tyson, 1992). Pentecostal historian, Vinson Synan, has chronicled Parham's rough start with pastoring and especially his strained relationship with the Methodist church. In his book, *The Holiness-Pentecostal Movement in the United States*, he states, "Parham seems to have had difficulty adjusting to ecclesiastical discipleship. Frequent disagreements with church officials over what he considered to be narrowness and sectarianism led within three years to a permanent break with the Methodist church. He also cultivated an anti-denominational view" (Synan, 1971).

By 1894 he was pastoring in Endora, Kansas. It's while in Endora that he began his fellowship and came under the influence of the Holiness movement (Tyson, 1992). In 1898, with nothing but pocket money and faith, Parham and his bride of two years, Eleanor Sarah ThistlethWaite, moved to Topeka, Kansas. There he started his famous Bethel Healing Ministries (Tyson, 1992; Valdez, 1980). His faith home, as he called the Bethel Healing Home, was for the ill and crippled who were too poor to pay for care and lodging. His concern was to provide a hospitable environment for those seeking divine healing (Tyson, 1992). Parham had come under the influence of one of the great faith healers of the day, John Alexander Dowie of Zion City, Illinois. In early 1900 he personally visited Dowie to see firsthand his work with the healing ministry. During the early part of that year he also visited faith healing and Holiness ministries in Cleveland, Chicago, and Shiloh, Maine (Tyson, 1992).

Upon his return to Topeka in October of 1900, Parham also started a Bible school. The college, like the healing home, was a faith-run venture and a labor of love. It was run by him and his wife, Sarah, who had now become the Reverend Sarah Parham (Tyson, 1992). The next years, from mid-1898 until mid-1901, would be the three most momentous years for the Parhams, according to author, John W. Ripley (Tyson, 1992).

Parham and his school published a bi-monthly paper called *The Apostolic Faith*. He filled the paper with testimonies of those who had been healed and with messages preached by himself and Mrs. Parham. Also in the paper Parham condemned established church policies to which he objected. In one editorial, he blasted the brand of faith-healing advocated by Mary Baker Eddy, founder of the Boston-based Christian Scientist Movement. He contended that Christian Science was all wrong because it maintained that death and disease were illusions. Parham declared that both were very real but that they required the services of an Apostolic faith healer like himself to effect cures (Tyson, 1992).

In October of 1900 Parham rented, for $40 a month, an elaborate two-story mansion that had been vacant but unfinished for a decade. The thirty-room mansion, designed after a European medieval castle but with Asian embellishments, had been built by eccentric real estate developer Erastus Stone in 1888 (Tyson, 1992). It sat on the outskirts of Topeka and was quickly dubbed Stone's Folly because it looked so bizarre (Tyson, 1992). The house had two towers with spires and balconies, resembling something out of the Arabian Nights, according to Paul Lovewell, a neighbor of Parham, who as a youth had watched it being built (Tyson, 1992). He said that its castle-like appearance added a sort of mystical atmosphere to the flat barren landscape (Tyson, 1992).

In 1898, after Erastus Stone's real estate company collapsed, he sold the house to a Robert Stone, a prominent Topeka attorney. The home was then leased out until September 1900, when Reverend Parham made an offer to rent the property. From October 1900 to July of 1901, the property would serve as the home for Parham's entire Bethel ministries operations. It would be from this location that Parham would mount his challenge to the Christian faith. As a result, Christianity would be changed forever. It was here that the first reported tongues speaking happened in the twentieth century. (Burgess, 1988).

Photo of John Alexander Dowie, founder of The Dowie Healing Ministry in Zion City, Illinois. This picture appears in, *Chalices of Gold*, by James L. Tyson.

The Topeka Revival

All Pentecostal histories of the twentieth century begin with an account of what happened with Parham and about thirty-five persons here at Topeka on January 1, 1901. Most Pentecostals consider the Topeka, Kansas revival to be the beginning of the modern era of Apostolic restoration (Tyson, 1992). Pentecostals around the planet, regardless of denominational ties, owe at the very least a debt of gratitude for the pioneering efforts of Charles F. Parham and the "Bethel-ites" in seeking a new and higher fellowship with God (Tyson, 1992).

A.C. Valdez, in his important work, *Fire On Azusa*, expresses succinctly what happened at the Topeka, Kansas revival: "On New Year's eve of 1900, forty students and seventy visitors gathered in the top room to pray and seek the Lord. Parham, who had been away on a speaking engagement, came in and gasped in surprise...the room was brighter than if lit by powerful electric lights... formed around a congregant's head, and a stream of exotic words poured out of her mouth... Behind the organ, Parham sank to his knees and, ...almost instantly, he began speaking in a tongue foreign to him. Soon all were speaking in languages which they had never before known or studied..." (Valdez, 1980). It would be this phenomenon of glossolalia which would set in motion the theology of twentieth-century Pentecostalism.

Initially Parham's Bethel school was besieged with reporters from cities all over the mid-west. It is reported they even brought with them professors of languages (Tyson, 1992). As Parham traveled he drew large crowds. Crusades were held all across Kansas in towns such as Galena, Mellville, Melrose, Baxter Springs, and Dorado Springs. His strong emphasis on divine healing drew people from all over. From 1901-1905 Parham was at the height of his success.

Parham Arrives in Houston

By 1905 the non-stop work and the strenuous travel regimen were taking a toll on Parham physically. He was having serious

The Parham family. This picture appears in *The Life and Ministry of William J. Seymour* by Larry Martin.

health problems. After the winter of 1904-1905 he left the midwest snows of Topeka to rest and recover with friends in the warm, sunny Houston Gulf Coast area (Nelson, 1988).

While in Houston in July and August of 1905, he was inspired to open a short-term Bible school in Houston. He rented the huge old Bryan Hall building at Fifth and Rusk (Valdez, 1980). In the daytime he would teach, and by night Parham and his team of students would parade down Main Street wearing spectacular clothing of the Holy Land, holding aloft a large banner emblazoned with the words Apostolic Faith Movement (Nelson, 1981). Once back at the Hall they would hold nightly services.

Among those attending the services was Lucy F. Farrow, the pastor of Seymour's black Holiness church in Houston. She was so taken with Parham that when he returned home to Kansas in August, she returned with him to serve as a governess for his five children (Nelson, 1981; Tyson, 1992). She asked her friend, William J. Seymour, to pastor the church in her absence. He accepted and pastored the congregation until she returned in October 1905 (Nelson, 1981).

While Seymour pastored the church in Mrs. Farrow's absence, he met Mrs. Neeley Terry. She was visiting family in Houston, and was from Los Angeles. Mrs. Terry, a former Baptist, was a recent convert to the Holiness movement. She had been exposed to the teachings of Phineas Bresee, a founder of the Church of the Nazarene. He had created a hospitable climate for the new tongues doctrine in Los Angeles as early as 1895. Bresee had been exposed to antecedents of Pentecostalism while on a trip to England in the early 1890's (Synan, 1971).

Starting his work at Peniel Mission, in the very poorest section of Los Angeles, Bresee was repeating Wesley's work of an earlier century in England by ministering to the disinherited of Los Angeles. His Nazarene followers were rapidly becoming the largest Holiness church in America.

Neeley Terry had been formally excommunicated from the Baptist church she attended in Los Angeles, because of her new persuasion toward Holiness. She, along with members of her

The Bethel Healing Home, the headquarters of Charles F. Parham in Topeka, Kansas.

Parham and part of his Apostolic band in Carthage, Missouri, circa 1905. This picture appears in *The Early Pentecostal Revival* by James L. Tyson.

This is a young Charles Fox Parham.
This photo appears in *Anointed to Serve* by William W. Menzies.

family, became members of a small Nazarene holiness mission in Los Angeles under the leadership of Mrs. Julia Hutchinson (Tinney, 1979).

In late October, Lucy Farrow returned to Houston with the Parham family. She again assumed the reins of the holiness mission there in Houston. She told Seymour about her Kansas experience, including the glowing account of having spoken in "tongues" (Nelson, 1981). She related to him that glossolalia was not simply a part of the early Christian church, but was intended for the present age as well (Nelson, 1981). Seymour became interested. When Reverend Parham announced that he would again open up the Bible school while he was in Houston, Seymour expressed a desire to attend.

However, the Jim Crow racial codes in place in Houston at this time prohibited African-Americans and whites from worshiping together. Seeing Seymour's eagerness and willingness to learn, Parham worked out a compromise that allowed Seymour to sit just outside the classroom beside the door, which Seymour would leave ajar. In this manner, Seymour attended classes every morning (Nelson, 1981; Valdez, 1982).

Parham would then use Seymour as he preached and visited in the black sections of Houston. They became friends, as much as was possible for the times and the conditions in which they lived. However, Pentecostal historian James Tinney points out that Parham and Seymour were not always on the best of terms. "They sometimes disagreed rather vociferously" (Tinney, 1978, p. 5). Parham did not believe in entire sanctification as a second, definite work of grace, while Seymour did. Parham also had very liberal ideas about permitting Christians to divorce and remarry (Tinney, 1978). Seymour did not believe in remarriage of divorced persons for any cause. He was also in disagreement with Parham about other sexual liberties. Further, Parham disliked much physical demonstration in worship service, and he ridiculed Seymour for encouraging "holy roller-isms" (Tinney, 1978). But the thing that Tinney says broke Seymour's heart and caused him to rebel against Parham was the white preacher's racial prejudice

(Tinney, 1978). Parham not only seated Black people separately in the rear of his meetings, but also prohibited interracial mingling at the altar afterwards (Nelson, 1981). Nelson gives this as the reason for Seymour not receiving the glossolalia experience while attending Parham's school in Houston.

Seymour Leaves Houston

Mrs. Neeley Terry returned to Los Angeles highly impressed with the pastoral and godly demeanor of William J. Seymour. She raved about his spiritual qualifications. Pastor Julia Hutchins and the small congregation were so impressed and inspired with the testimony of Mrs. Terry that they quickly raised the train fare and sent for Seymour (Tinney, 1978). They had been relying on the leadership of Mrs. Hutchinson and others. Tired of spontaneous leadership from meeting to meeting, they decided that it was now time to designate one acknowledged leader (Nelson, 1981). Seymour, who was having a strained relationship with Reverend Parham, sought his blessing, but accepted the invitation as a mission from God himself. He resolved to leave Houston without delay (Nelson, 1981).

About his call to go to Los Angeles he later wrote:

It was the divine call that brought me from Houston to Los Angeles. The Lord put it on the heart of one of the saints in Los Angeles to write to me that she felt the Lord wanted me to come there, and I felt that was the leading of the Lord. The Lord provided the means and I came to take charge of a mission on Santa Fe Street (Tinney, 1978, p. 6).

Excitedly, Brother Seymour was ready to embark upon what would become one of the most eventful periods in his life.

Racism is an integral, permanent, and indestructible component of this society.
> *Faces at the Bottom of the Well*
> Derrick Bell (1992)

CHAPTER 6
ON TO LOS ANGELES

While in route to Los Angeles, Seymour made many stops to visit holiness missions which had sprung up across the country. One of the well-known missions that he stopped at was in Denver, Colorado; it was the mid-point of the trip. There he attended The Pillar of Fire Church, pastored by Mrs. Alma White. Mrs. White (1862-1946) was the first holiness white woman bishop in the country (Dupree, 1996). This honor was bestowed upon her in 1918 by her church. She was against the emerging tongues movement, but was an ardent follower of the Holiness Movement.

In 1906 William J. Seymour visited her church and Bible school. Mrs. White leaves one of the most discouraging descriptions of Brother Seymour that has come to us. She called Seymour, "an untidy person ... wearing no collar ... son of perdition" (Nelson, 1981, p. 83). He was branded by her as ... "an instrument of Satan..." (Nelson, 1981, p. 83). It is a well established fact that Mrs. White's descriptions were shaded by her prejudicial opinion of colored people and the Pentecostal movement (Dupree, 1996). In the 1916 book, *Demons and Tongues*, she writes that Seymour's prayers conjured up feelings of "serpents and slimy creatures" (Dupree, 1996, p. 536). She said that Seymour was demon-possessed (Nelson, 1981, p. 83). She later said of the Azusa Street Mission, that it was located in one of the "worse slums" in Los Angeles (Nelson, 1981, p. 83). She went on to say that the scenes of kissing and familiarity between the sexes and races was the "...climax of demon worship" (Nelson, 1981, p. 83). She wrote that Satan himself had chosen Seymour to lead this movement of fleshly lust because he was a colored man, and as such, a descendant of Ham, cursed by Noah for lack of respect and a fleshly bent. She surmised that for this reason God had ordered Joshua to utterly destroy the Canaanites; descendants of Ham.

Alma White, pastor of the Denver church, Pillar of Fire. Collection of Larry Martin, *The Life and Ministry of William J. Seymour.*

Douglas Nelson, points out in his dissertation of Seymour that probably White's strong opposition and anger to Seymour, as well as Pentecostalism, came from the fact that her husband, Kent, joined the Pentecostal ranks and left her around 1909 (Nelson, 1981). She had also tried to lead a mission in Los Angeles that had been unsuccessful. She always blamed Angelenos for rejecting her. In her later writings, she commented of Seymour "... of all the religious fakers and tramps... he excelled them all" (Synan, 1971, pp. 119-120). It must be stated also that years later she wrote for, and gave her support to the resurgent Ku Klux Klan (Nelson, 1981).

Morton Kelsey, in his book on speaking in tongues, also writes about Seymour's personal appearance. Kelsey says he was unprepossessing in his manner, and rather careless about his person (Kelsey, 1964). Kelsey, like most writers of Pentecostal history, had used White's unflattering description of Seymour as the basis for this assertion.

Brother Seymour arrived in Los Angeles in April of 1906 after a journey of ninety-six hours (Nelson, 1981). In 1906 California was rocked by two of the most devastating earthquakes to hit the world. A physical earthquake tore San Francisco asunder, and in early April the spirit of revival set Los Angeles aflame. It would become the center of the twentieth-century worldwide Pentecostal Revival.

Los Angeles City

In 1906 Los Angeles was a city of true American diversity, the kind of diversity that conjures up the melting pot ideal. The city was founded in 1781 by Felipe DeNeve. He served as the Spanish governor of California from 1775 to 1782. DeNeve originated the idea of establishing a pueblo on the land where Los Angeles now lies. He recommended the idea to the Viceroy of Mexico, who obtained the approval of King Carlos III of Spain (Berry, 1995; Nelson 1981). With a population comprised largely of settlers from Mexico, El Pueblo de Nuestra Senora la Reina de Los Angeles de Porciuncula (the town of Our Lady the Queen of the

Early turn of the century view of Main Street in Los Angeles, California, circa 1891. Courtesy of L.A. Times Library, Los Angeles Public Library.

Angeles of Porciuncula) was thus founded on September 4, 1781 (Berry, 1995).

On September 4, 1781 eleven families of settlers arrived that consisted of forty-four persons. These included twenty-two adults and twenty-two children -- two Whites, sixteen Indians, and twenty-six Negroes. This was the beginning of California.

After California entered the Union in 1850, following the war of 1847 between the U.S. and Mexico, the discovery of gold caused a dramatic explosion in the state's population. In 1876, the Southern Pacific railroad reached Los Angeles, which increased the population even more. By 1900, there were well over one hundred thousand people living in Los Angeles (Singleton, 1977). Los Angeles, by all accounts, quickly became the fastest growing American city.

Even in its infancy Los Angeles, was something of an obstreperous, headstrong city. Those who sired what was to become one of the most alluring, repelling, attractive, disappointing, magically baffling metropolises of the world poured into its life-stream a conglomerate of good and evil, noble and infamous. However varied the basic motivations of those early pioneers, one thing was shared: boundless optimism about the future.

The City of Angels, as the early Spaniards called her, by the 1890's had become the foremost city of southern California (Henry, 1955). Many of its pioneer-spirited residents had followed the gleam of the mid-Century gold rush. This city of the future was a dream city of many shapes and patterns to as many different people. There were those who saw the city for what she really was: a composite of human beings at a fork in the road.

By the 1890's, the city was at a crossroad experience of eternal souls making eternal decisions with eternal implications not only for itself but for generations to come. Methodist-Episcopal clergyman, J. W. Brier, who reached Los Angeles by oxcart in 1852, already sensed the city's spiritual hardness of heart (Henry, 1955). He wrote an 1881 *Los Angeles Times* article arguing that the community was "rapidly developing into a highly immoral town" (Henry, 1955, p. 22).

In the 1890's less than one-sixth of the inhabitants were actually in the churches. If this picture kindled concern for the unchurched already within the city's boundaries, how overwhelming it must have been for the families streaming daily from all directions into the tumultuous Los Angeles vortex of the 1890's. The completed Southern Pacific and Santa Fe lines spilled more people in less time into the bustling city than had come in all the decades before.

In 1906 Los Angeles was experiencing a population annual growth rate of fifteen percent yearly (Tyson, 1992). City planners were deeply concerned about the demands of such growth. One major concern was the need for water. Los Angeles is situated in the middle of what is actually a desert. Even today water is still a major concern at times.

When William arrived in 1906, the city was a place of diverse nationalities, including Japanese, African-Americans, Chinese, Russians, Greeks, Mexicans, Native Americans and Anglo-Saxons. It had a population of 250,000. It was indeed a bustling metropolis.

Small Spanish pueblos of adobe and one-story frame cottages had changed into an extensive city of brick and stone block residences. Los Angeles was the first city in the nation to abandon gas for electric street lights (Henry, 1955). It had become one of the best illuminated cities in the United States. It also boasted an extensive network of graded and graveled streets, cement and asphalt sidewalks, an internal sewer system, six public parks, large hotels, two handsome theaters, The Grand Opera House, the Los Angeles Theater, a huge courthouse, and a city hall (Henry, 1955). It seemed a veritable Canaan, flowing with milk and honey.

But there was much more as well. The city was crowded with the faces of those seeking: faces of children and of men tense with the ruthlessness of frontier life. Lives upon lives tense with the pains of material and spiritual hunger. For this reason, by the 1890's, churches and missions were springing up all over the

Frank Bartleman, 1906. It was his accurate journals and diaries that left the well-preserved history of The Azusa Street revival.

place. Quietly, in December of 1890, one of the most famous missions of these times would organize, the Pacific Gospel Union, now known as the Union Rescue Mission (Henry, 1955). It would be this same environment that would also give birth to the famed Azusa Street Mission a decade later.

Los Angeles was teeming with all kinds of ideological and religious experimentation. A journalist, Frank Bartleman, would document many of the religious ideologies of the day in the Times. He would eventually become a Pentecostal, converted while covering the Azusa Street Revival. He would go on to document the first eyewitness account of the Revival, and write the book, *How Pentecost Came To Los Angeles: How It Was In The Beginning*, in 1925 (Synan, 1980). This book was republished in 1980 under the title, *Azusa Street*, by Logos International Press, Plainfield, N.J.

The city of Los Angeles, with its rapidly growing population of such diverse people, cultures, and ethnicity, was a laboratory for the new and different, much as it is today. It became the cradle of the twentieth-century Pentecostal tradition.

The Spiritual Climate in Los Angeles

Around the turn of the Century, the desire to restore primitive Christianity was sweeping the country (Synan, 1975). Los Angeles would participate as a major center in this latest renewal of Protestant history (Nelson, 1981; Synan, 1975; Raboteau, 1997).

Mrs. Neely Terry, the person who had invited Seymour to come to Los Angeles, was a converted Baptist. She had been exposed to the teachings of Phineas Bresee, the Los Angeles founder of the Church of the Nazarene. He had created a suitable climate for the new tongues doctrine in Los Angeles as early as 1895. Bresee had been exposed to Pentecostalism while on a trip to England and Wales a decade before the Azusa Street revival (Synan, 1975).

Starting his work at the Peniel mission, in the very poorest section of the city, Bresee was repeating Wesley's work of an earlier century in England, by ministering to the disinherited. His Nazarene followers rapidly became the largest Holiness church in America. The Peniel Hall, which seated 900, was a Holiness center, which shared in all aspects of spiritual life.

Other spiritual leaders living in Los Angeles also contributed to the atmosphere which would eventually create the Azusa Street Revival. They included: Elmer Fisher of the Glendale Baptist Church, Alfred Garr, pastor of the Burning Bush Mission and a leader within the Metropolitan Holiness Association; William Manley, known as the tent preacher for his many tent revivals around the Los Angeles area; Arthur Osterberg of the Full Gospel Church; and Joseph Smale, pastor of the prestigious First Baptist Church who had personally met Evan Roberts of the Welsh Revival. It was Roberts, along with Phineas Bresee, who would actually introduce Los Angeles to the movement in 1895 (Synan,

Phineas F. Bresee, a founder of The Church of the Nazarene, taken from *Phineas F. Bresee, A Prince In Israel* by E. A. Girvin.

1975; Shumway, 1916; Bartleman, 1925). Smale, like so many of these pastors was forced to resign from his church when he started to espouse the new doctrine of Pentecostalism. He started The New Testament Church. It would play a prominent role in the early days of twentieth-century Pentecostal history (Synan, 1975; Shumway, 1916; Bartleman, 1925).

William Seymour Arrives

According to author and professor of Pentecostal history, Mel Robeck, William arrived in Los Angeles in February of 1906.[27] In April of 1906 he preached his first sermon to the mission on Santa Fe Street that was pastored by Mrs. Julia Hutchinson. Sister Hutchinson had formerly been a Baptist. She began teaching holiness and sanctification as separate works of grace in addition to a born-again experience. As other members of that congregation began to accept her teachings she was expelled.

She opened her own mission. A relative of hers, Neeley Terry, who had met William while in Houston the year before, told of Seymour's gifts as a preacher. He was immediately sent for, because Mrs. Hutchinson had wanted a male to assist her in the work.

William was warmly accepted by the small holiness assembly. With eagerness they waited to hear the short, stocky, one-eyed black preacher (Ewart, 1975) from Texas espouse the word of God. The text of his first sermon was taken from Acts. 2:4.[28] He preached it with conviction and power even though he hadn't yet spoken in tongues (Synan, 1971). The message was too new, and too disturbing and controversial, for these simple holiness people who had not yet accepted tongues as a doctrine of the church. When William returned for the Sunday night service he found that Sister Hutchinson had padlocked the doors (Tinney, 1978).

Pastor Hutchinson had decided to put an end to the new talk. After a debate with a delegation of Nazarene ministers and others associated with the local Holiness Association, Seymour was barred from further activities at the church. What a devastating

William J. Seymour, circa 1912. From the collection of Rev. Franklin C. Showell, Baltimore Maryland.

blow William must have experienced. He had come all the way from Texas; he knew no one in Los Angeles, he had no money, and now his only friends had locked him out.

Brother Seymour had shared dinner that Sunday with a Brother Lee (Ewart, 1975). Brother Lee, after returning with Seymour and seeing the door locked, ... "solely out of Christian courtesy invited him to his home" (Tinney, 1978, p. 5). The Lees, being members of the Peniel Mission, didn't believe in Pentecostalism. After days of praying about Brother Seymour's new doctrine, a Mr. and Mrs. Richard Asbury, friends of the Lees, being more sympathetic to Seymour's new doctrine, invited him to stay in their home.

Bonnie Brae Street Beginning

The Asburys lived at 312 North Bonnie Brae Street (Ewart, 1975; Valdez, 1980; Synan, 1971). The house was situated on a hill with about sixteen steps leading up to the rather large porch. The house was a simple large dwelling in the Victorian architectural style of the day.[29] The spacious living room was used to conduct nightly prayer services.

It was on April 9, 1906, that the miracle of Pentecost happened (Ewart, 1975). Brother Lee came to the Asbury's for Brother Seymour to lay hands on him. He had experienced a vision of receiving the Holy Ghost. Originally Lee felt that he couldn't accept the third blessing doctrine.[30] For this reason Seymour was utterly delighted when Lee appeared at the prayer meeting (Ewart, 1975). Lee burst in the room, threw up his arms and began to speak in tongues. Instantly the power of God fell on six others as well and they all began to speak in tongues (Ewart, 1975; Foster, 1961). The revival had started.

Among those receiving the new birth was Jennie Evans Moore, who would later become William Seymour's wife (Ewart, 1975; Tinney, 1978). It was reported that Sister Moore, after receiving the Holy ghost, went over to the piano, and under the anointing of the Spirit proceeded to play. It must be stated here that she had never played the piano before[31] (MacRoberts, 1988).

An original view of the Bonnie Brae Street house, home of the original Seymour revival as it appeared in 1906. The picture was taken from, *The History of the Pentecostal Assemblies of the World*, by Morris Golder.

The news traveled quickly and people came from seemingly everywhere. By the next morning it was impossible to get near the house (Ewart, 1975). When people would get near the house, many would fall under the anointing power of God. For three days many were healed and saved. The crowds grew immensely. Seymour was forced to begin to preach on the porch (Tinney, 1978). From the porch the crowds spilled onto the streets, and the street then became their temple. It was on April 12 that William J. Seymour received the gift of the Holy Ghost (Ewart, 1975).

A search went forth for a larger site. It was obvious that a place in a non-residential area was needed. The area had to be tolerant of the new type of Pentecostal services. Sometimes the services would continue all night long with people loudly praising the Lord. The meetings were characterized by men and women shouting, dancing, weeping, falling to the floor, and, of course, speaking in tongues.

A later view of 312 Bonnie Brae Street, site of the first Seymour revival in Los Angeles. The house was owned by the Richard Asbury family, circa 1979. Picture appeared in "Such A Time As This" by Douglas Nelson.

A more modern look at the 312 Bonnie Brae Street house where the first Seymour revival took place, circa, 1992. From the collection of Rufus Sanders.

The piano in the Bonnie Brae Street house. Appears as it did when the revival started in 1906, circa 1992. Collection of Rufus Sanders.

The entire city began to hear of the movement (Ewart, 1975).

And as we walk, we must make the pledge that we shall march ahead. We cannot turn back...and we will not be satisfied until justice rolls down like waters and righteousness like a mighty stream.... I am not unmindful that some of you have come here out of great trials and tribulations...I say to you today, my friends, that in spite of the difficulties and frustrations of the moment I still have a dream. It is a dream rooted in the American dream.... This will be the day when all of God's children will be able to sing with new meaning.... My country 'tis of thee, sweet land of liberty of thee I sing...Land where my fathers died, land of the Pilgrim's pride, from every mountainside, let freedom ring.... When we let freedom ring...when we let it ring from every village and every hamlet, from every state and every city, we will be able to speed up that day when all of God's children, black men and white men, Jews and Gentiles, Protestants and Catholics, will be able to join hands and sing in the words of the old Negro spiritual.... Free at last! Free at last! Thank God Almighty, we are free at last!

> Excerpts from the "I Have A Dream" speech -- Dr. Martin Luther King, Jr. (1963)

CHAPTER 7
AZUSA STREET
The Work Begins

After a diligent search for a new location, 312 Azusa Street was found. Azusa Street lay in what was then the industrial heart of early twentieth-century Los Angeles. It was surrounded by the growing Black community of Los Angeles. The new meeting place had at one time been a Methodist Church. The First African Methodist Episcopal Church of Los Angeles had resided there in the 1880's. It was a two-story building with an outside stairway leading to the front door, a pitched roof, and attached steeple. The church met here until 1904. In that year a fire broke out. When the building was re-occupied by Seymour in 1906, the steeple had been removed, replaced by a flat-top roof that is seen in all remaining photos of the Azusa Street Mission.

Proud Legacy of Biddy Mason

The land that the First African Methodist Episcopal Church was set on had been originally owned by a black woman named Biddy Mason. Ms. Mason had purchased the land for $250 in 1866. The land purchased by Ms. Mason today is worth $24 million, and houses a shopping arcade and high-rise parking garage in the middle of a tree-shaded mini-park in downtown Los Angeles. As testimony and commemoration to her contributions, the park was named Biddy Mason Park in her honor in 1991.

Ms. Mason, a one-time Mississippi slave who fought to win her freedom, became a major Los Angeles land owner and philanthropist in the late 1800's. It was her money that built the First African Methodist Episcopal Church in Los Angeles. She had been born a slave in 1818; she grew up to become a nurse and midwife. She came from Salt Lake City to Los Angeles with her

The Azusa Street sign as it appears today in Los Angeles.

Early view of Azusa Street Mission, circa 1906. Part of *The Life and Ministry of William J. Seymour* **by Larry Martin.**

Mormon masters in 1848, walking across the continent behind their wagon train.

Upon arrival in California, she learned that it was a free state. In 1856, she went to court, and won her freedom. For the next several years she saved her wages from her midwife and nursing work to buy property between Spring Street and Broadway. This would include the Azusa Street area.

In the years that followed, "Biddy Mason's place" became known as a daycare center and orphanage, and as the general meeting area for the city's African-American population. She became a living legend. She died in 1891 and is buried in Evergreen Cemetery in Boyle Heights.[32] When the First African Methodist Episcopal Church moved to West Adams and Hoover it sold the building to The Saint Stephens AME Church, which leased it to Seymour and his fledgling band of believers in 1904.

Cleaning of the Temple

The new church was, according to Dr. Nelson, a barn like, ram-shackle building (Nelson, 1981). The bottom floor had a dirt floor, and had been recently used as a livery stable. The upper portion had been used as living quarters for nearby factory workers. It had also been used as a storage place.

The Saint Stephens Methodist Church had moved out in 1903 (Nelson, 1981). The church's gothic stained-glass windows was removed at that time. The exterior stairway had also been removed and the stained-glass windows had been replaced with regular ones. The building was leased to Seymour for $8.00 per month. It was capable of holding as many as 900 persons.[33] Next to this building, ironically, was a tombstone shop.

The task of cleaning 312 Azusa Street was formidable. But when it was accomplished, the newly white-washed building quickly became the spiritual headquarters of American Pentecostalism. The old ram-shackle building was prepared with sawdust spread on the dirt floor. Planks nailed to legs were used as benches. A pulpit was made out of two wooden shoe boxes.

When the renovation was completed, the revival began imme-

A 1904 picture of the Azusa Street Mission. The building had been used as a livery stable. A "For Sale" sits on the building. This is just prior to it being rented by William Seymour. This picture is from *The Early Pentecostal Revival* by James L. Tyson. It is the earliest known photograph of the Azusa Street Mission.

diately and lasted for three years uninterrupted. One man declared, "When I got within three blocks of the meeting house, I could feel the atmosphere charge" (Ewart, 1975, p. 79). The closer he came, according to this person, the stronger the supernatural feeling became. He stated that when he opened the door, he seemed to be ushered into a holy, sequestered place; a veritable Holy of Holies (Ewart, 1975).

All kinds of people came to scoff, but many came to pray, and some who would come to scoff stayed to pray. The *Los Angeles Times* ran a story about the revival on April 18, 1906. Its headline read... "Weird Babel of Tongues". The article went on to say... "a breathing of strong utterances and mouthing, a creed which it would seem no sane mortal could understand." As national attention had come to the new Pentecostal movement, pilgrims and onlookers arrived from the world over (Tinney, 1978). People of all colors, races, creeds, and religions came to Los Angeles.

Seymour: The Man, The Leader

In the center of all this excitement was William J. Seymour. By some accounts, this one-eyed black man from Texas was anything but the likely choice for a leader. It was said that Seymour was so meek and plain that he was anything but a dynamic leader. Arthur G. Osterberg, pastor of The Independent Full Gospel Church in Los Angeles at the time, said of Seymour, "that with no more emotionalism than a post...he was no arm-waving thunder by any stretch of the imagination..." (Nelson, 1981, p. 82).

Seymour was no authoritarian and he had no real organization about him. He waged no massive advertising campaigns. He had no musical accompaniment. He lifted no offering. He had no guest speakers or evangelists. Often no one ran the services at all. Most of the time Brother Seymour, who had taken the title of Elder Seymour by now, could be found in front with his face in the shoe box crates in prayer (Ewart, 1975). Seymour viewed his role as that of one who kept the place in order (Ewart, 1975).

But Seymour had a commanding, charismatic personality that demanded attention and respect. He was accused by some of being a hypnotist, able to command with his starry-optic eye. But in the midst of criticism and attacks on his person by his enemies, he maintained his loyal following.

It was told to Frank Ewart, an Azusa Street veteran, how Elder Seymour would tell seekers to ask definite things of the Lord: "Be emphatic, ask!" (Ewart, 1975). Altar calls or urging were never needed because people would rise and run to the altar continuously during the service. Seekers were sometimes taken upstairs to a long room appropriately called the Pentecostal "upper room" (Ewart, 1975).[34] This room was used also for daily Bible study. This floor also contained living quarters for those who were homeless. In this new brotherhood, all racial barriers were broken. What a strange and glorious sight to behold in the days of Plessy

Biddy Mason, the black founder of modern Los Angeles. This photo is taken from *The Life and Ministry of William J. Seymour* by Larry Martin.

vs. Ferguson and Jim Crow: whites and blacks in America on their knees together side by side praying for a oneness.

Faith-Based Operations

The church was operated solely on free-will offerings. It was said that Brother Seymour would walk around with five and ten dollars sticking out of his pockets, placed there by his parishioners and unnoticed by him (Ewart, 1975). It was reported that food arrived daily -- no questions were asked, no payments made; everyone merely thanked God.

Elder Seymour eventually put together, out of need, a very loose church organizational structure. The mission's members began to call it The Apostolic Faith Movement. Like his mentor, Reverend Charles F. Parham, Seymour published a free newspaper called *The Apostolic Faith*. Its initial printing of 5,000 copies grew to 50,000 by the end of 1906 (Nelson, 1981).

The mission began to send out men and women missionaries both in the United States and abroad. Glenn Cook, one of the original Azusa Street witnesses, spread the Gospel across the United States as one of the first evangelists from the mission (Ewart, 1975). A.G. Garr and his wife went to India from the mission to spread the Word (Ewart, 1975). From there they would travel to China and eventually settled in Hong Kong. William Seymour reported in *The Apostolic Faith* newspaper that in 1907 Lucy Farrow, who had come with him to Los Angeles, was made missionary to Liberia (Dupree, 1996). She would be joined there by Sister Julia Hutchinson.

The pioneers of Azusa Street stood firm for three years as the revival went on literally non-stop. The manifestations of God were always present. Seymour endured opposition, doubt, fanaticism, and criticism which threatened to stop the work. In many instances Los Angeles holiness churches would close their own services and in mass come to the Azusa Street mission.

A picture of what the Mission looked like when it served as the first African-Methodist Church in Los Angeles prior to 1900. The original steps are visible. This picture appeared in the dissertation, "For Such A Time As This" by Douglas Nelson, 1981

Seymour Under Attack

As the meetings grew in size, so did the criticism. Many felt that the meetings were becoming nothing but side shows of devil-inspired emotionalism. Some felt the services were too extreme even for traditional holiness people. A movement emerged within the mission to usurp the position of Elder Seymour. It was led by critics who said Seymour was no longer capable of leading a growing organization. But Seymour's lack of education and his skin color were probably the primary reasons for this opposition. Before long, spiritualists and mediums from the occult communities began to attend and promote their religious attitudes. Seymour tried to control their enthusiasm and emotionalism, but to no avail. He even attempted to de-emphasize speaking in

Another view of Azusa Street Mission, *The Life and Ministry of William J. Seymour*, Larry Martin, circa 1907.

Another view of Azusa Street Mission, circa 1907.

A 1906, April 18 copy of the *Los Angeles Times*. The lead story is about the Azusa Street Revival.

A *Los Angeles Times*, July 23, 1906, copy about the continued Pentecostal Revival in Los Angeles.

William J. Seymour, circa 1912. This portrait is a part of the collection of Franklin C. Showell, Baltimore, Maryland.

The original Azusa Street Revival Committee, circa 1906. Public domain.

William Seymour with some of the original members of the Azusa Street Mission, circa 1906.

William J. Seymour and Mrs. Jennie M. Seymour, circa 1910. This photo appears in the dissertation of Douglas Nelson, "For Such A Time As This".

tongues in an effort to regain control (Ewart, 1975). Some outsiders declared that the entire thing consisted of talking in tongues and was inspired by the devil.

Alma White was so upset by seeing a colored woman with her arms around a white man's neck praying for him that she branded Seymour an "instrument of satan". Concerned by these developments and threatened with the loss of control over the movement he had founded, Seymour took the dramatic step of sending for Reverend Parham (Synan, 1971).

Enter Parham

Parham did not come directly to Los Angeles, but decided to go to Zion City, Illinois first. In Zion City he came to the aid of another faltering holiness movement headed by Reverend Alexander Dowie. Parham advised Seymour on how to handle the "foreign spirits" and told him to continue until he came. Parham was recognized, not only by Seymour but the entire Pentecostal movement, as a man of wisdom and experience (MacRoberts, 1988).

Parham visited in the fall of 1906. He received a warm welcome. He preached and proceeded to put things in order. He was shocked by the "Holy Rollerism" he saw (Nelson, 1981). "When he reached Azusa", writes Nelson, "he recoiled in disgust at what he saw: "...blacks and whites intermingling against every accepted custom of American society" (Nelson, 1981, p. 96).

Parham said that to his utter surprise and astonishment he found conditions even worse than he had anticipated. There were two reasons for this, according to Nelson. First, he observed various charismas being demonstrated too openly by the congregation to suit him. For example, some worshipers were falling to the ground in apparent trances, believing themselves to be under some unusual manifestation of divine spiritual power. Parham rebuked the congregation for what he described as "animalism" (MacRoberts, 1988, p. 60). In his later writings, Parham claimed that at the Azusa mission people were taught to yield to any force...hypnotic influence...spooks, false spirits and demons

(MacRoberts, 1988, p. 60).

Parham said in his autobiography...

> I have seen meetings where all crowded together around the altar, and laying across one another like hogs, blacks and whites mingling; this should be enough to bring a blush of shame to devils, let alone angels, and yet all this was charged to the Holy Spirit (Parham, 1944, p. 83).

One report described Azusa as sometimes resembling a forest of fallen timbers.

The second condition that shocked Parham was the unusual degree of social and racial integration at the Azusa Street Mission. Like Alma White, Parham found this completely unacceptable. Like Ms. White, Parham had ties to the Ku Klux Klan (MacRoberts, 1988), and he objected strongly to racial mixing or mingling during the worship at the altar. While in Houston, Parham had followed strict segregation in his church. Blacks were always seated at the rear of the church and were refused participation in altar calls. Parham stated that he believed that the greatest sin of humanity was the mixing of the races (Nelson, 1981). In his view, it was for this that divine judgment had unleashed the flood of the Old Testament (MacRoberts, 1988; Nelson, 1981).

Inevitably, Seymour and Parham clashed over this issue. Seymour believed that the Azusa renewal was true Christianity, a renewal where all barriers of race, color, gender, class and nationality were in his view, divinely abolished. Frank Bartleman, the journalist who chronicled the Azusa revival wrote, "The color line was washed away in the blood" (Bartleman, 1980, p. 58).

At first Parham tried to persuade Seymour to resign and turn the reins over to him. However, The Azusa congregation rejected Parham's racism and his claim to leadership, and Parham was asked to leave. Parham withdrew from Azusa and until December ran a mission in the Los Angeles YMCA. His work had failed (MacRoberts, 1988; Nelson, 1981). Along with charges of racial intolerance, Parham also faced accusations of homosexuality from Seymour and other critics (MacRoberts, 1988). When Parham returned to Texas he was charged with homosexual conduct. His ministry never recovered (MacRoberts, 1988).

Iain MacRoberts reported that Parham, shamed, outcast, and defeated, left to search for Noah's Ark (MacRoberts, 1988). Until his death in 1929, Parham continued his relationship with the Ku Klux Klan, which he referred to as "those splendid men" (MacRoberts, 1988, p. 62). For the rest of his life Parham denounced the Azusa Street movement and William Joseph Seymour.

Seymour's Marriage Controversy

In 1908 Seymour married Jennie Evans Moore. She had been the first person to receive the new birth at Bonnie Brae Street. Nelson reports that on May 13, 1908 Seymour was married to the beautiful Moore, known for her intellect among the black people (Nelson, 1981).

It is said that when asked her race, while applying for marriage license, she gave "Ethiopian" as her answer. The Seymours moved into the upstairs quarters of the Azusa Street mission. She turned her home, which was just down the street from the Bonnie Brae Street mission, over to her relatives.

Nelson implies that some kind of personal relationship had developed between either Clara Lum or Florence Crawford and Seymour. Ms. Lum and Ms. Crawford, both white women, served as leaders in the Azusa Street mission. From just before his marriage in May, it is clear that some crisis developed within the mission organization that was a turning point in Seymour's influence as the leader of the worldwide movement. Ithiel Clemmons, a past president of the Society for Pentecostal Studies, in an 1981 address before the Society in Charlotte, NC, during their eleventh annual meeting, states that the possible consideration of an interracial marriage, by Seymour could have precipitated this controversy (Clemmons, 1981).

After Seymour's marriage to Jennie Moore in May of 1908, Clara Lum, who was the editor of Seymour's newsletter, took the

The Bishop C. H. Mason, founder of The Church of God In Christ, Inc. Public domain.

Clara Lum, original Azusa Street Revival Committee member, along with Florence Crawford, took the Azusa Street mailing list and moved to Portland, Oregon. She was linked romantically to William Seymour. This picture is in the public domain.

Rev. Florence Crawford, founder of The Apostolic Faith, Portland, Oregon. It was Rev. Crawford who took the Azusa Street mailing list from Seymour and along with Clara Lum fled to Portland. This photo appears in *The Apostolic Faith: An Historical Account*.

Pentecostal Concept of Salvation

	Stage 1 First Blessing	Stage 2 Second Blessing	Stage 3 Third Blessing
Original Holiness View	Conversion, also called repentance	Sanctification, distinct from conversion	
Parham/ Seymour View	Conversion	Sanctification	Baptism of Spirit, speaking in tongues
Durham's View	Conversion	Baptism of Spirit, speaking in tongues is synonymous with sanctification which is understood also as a continuing life process	

mailing list for the newspaper, and abruptly moved to Portland, Oregon. There she joined with another former Azusa Street associate, Florence Crawford, and they started their own paper (Nelson, 1981).

Clemmons reports that Seymour, just before deciding to marry Jennie Moore, had turned to his friend and mentor, C.H. Mason, for advice. Mason warned Seymour against an interracial marriage, given the makeup of his congregation (Clemmons, 1981).

It appears that whatever Seymour's original intentions were, he married Ms. Moore, but his decision also forced Ms. Lum to leave. With Ms. Lum's exit went the national mailing list, which was crucial to the livelihood of the mission (Nelson, 1981). The newly wedded Seymours went to Portland to retrieve the list, but to no avail (Nelson, 1981). Douglas Nelson reports that with the passing of the newspapers from the control of Seymour and the

Azusa Mission, an era ended at Los Angeles (Nelson, 1981). From this point on the Pentecostal Movement changed from one where there was no color line to one in which the color line was ever more tightly policed.

The Revival Comes To An End

The next problem to plague Seymour's Azusa Street Mission was the introduction of several new doctrines. In 1911, the "Finish Work of Calvary" theology was first preached (Ewart, 1975). This doctrine, though not accepted by Seymour, would do much to make Pentecostalism something more than another Los Angeles religious cult.

Prior to 1911, Pentecostals and Holiness people believed in the multiple works of grace theory: salvation, sanctification, and tongues. The "Finished Work of Calvary" doctrine was first preached by William Durham, a prominent ex-Baptist Holiness pastor from Chicago (Ewart, 1975). He, like so many others, had received the Holy Ghost at the mission under the anointing of William J. Seymour. At the time he received the Holy Ghost, Seymour, under the power of prophecy, declared that Durham would preach with the power of God.

When Durham came back to Los Angeles in 1910, after his initial visit in 1907, he was preaching that sanctification was a scriptural experience. It was a gradual advancement that one made after having the Holy Ghost. It was growth in the grace and knowledge of Jesus. The new doctrine, however, upset the unity within the new movement.

Since most of the original Pentecostal leaders had been prominent in the holiness movement, it seemed natural for them to maintain the idea of sanctification as a "second blessing" which cleansed the seeker from "inbred sin," thus preparing him for the Holy Spirit, yet another step in the salvation process. Baptist converts thought of Christian experience as involving only two steps, conversion and sanctification (See chart).

The individual who became the leader of this new doctrinal interpretation of salvation was William H. Durham of Chicago,

Illinois. He would question the second blessing theory. Durham had traveled to the Azusa Mission in 1907, and he returned in 1911 to share his new understanding of Pentecostal doctrine.

The controversy began with a sermon he preached at a Chicago convention in 1910 (Showell, 1976). There he sought to "nullify the blessing of sanctification as a second definite work of grace." Calling his new doctrine "The Finished Work", Durham called for an entirely new principle which assigned sanctification to the act of conversion based on the "finished work of Calvary." Denying the Wesleyan concept of a "residue of sin" in the believer, he taught that one was perfectly sanctified at conversion and had no need for a second blessing. According to Durham the Holy Spirit sanctifies you. Since Durham's teaching cut directly across the accepted view of the Pentecostals with "holiness background," a great controversy ensued which ultimately divided the movement into differing theological camps.

Upon Durham's return to Los Angeles, he found that, because of the internal problems, the glory of the Azusa Street Mission had been transferred to another mission across town called the Upper Room Mission, pastored by Elmer Fisher (Ewart, 1975). Though Seymour was not in town, Durham was permitted to preach at the Azusa Mission. He preached the "Finished Work" doctrine and the Mission quickly began to fill again. The messages were powerful, though many Pentecostal worshipers rejected the message in the same way that Holiness people had rejected Pentecostalism earlier. The Upper Room Mission membership became divided over the new issue, with their pastor creating yet another mission.

Hearing about the uproar, Seymour quickly returned to Los Angeles from his Evangelistic tour, and rejected the new "Finished Work" doctrine. He padlocked the door to prevent Brother Durham from preaching (Ewart, 1975). But it was too late, the seed had already been planted. Durham quickly secured another building and opened his own ministry, preaching to large, ecstatic crowds nightly. Seymour, however, never accepted the new doctrine and the Azusa Mission began to decline in atten-

Another early picture of the Azusa Street Mission with William Seymour out in front, circa 1906.

Rev. William Durham, the formulator of the Finished Work of Calvary doctrine. This picture appears in *The Life and Ministry of William J. Seymour* by Larry Martin, circa 1910.

Rev. Charles Lowe was given the church begun by Seymour in Franklin, Virginia, circa 1910. This picture appears in *The Life and Ministry of William J. Seymour* by Larry Martin.

dance and popularity. Many whites departed, leaving the Mission totally in the hands of African-American congregation members.

The Last Days of William Seymour

William continued to lead what was left of the Azusa Street Mission. He now began to preach that he would never die (Crawford, 1965). For a while, he was a traveling evangelist. Clemmons places Seymour in Harlem and East Orange, New Jersey in the early 1920's (1921-22) (Clemmons, 1981). It was during that time that Mason and Seymour met each other for the last time.

Seymour became the founder and head of an association called The Azusa Street Mission Churches on April 24, 1907 (Dupree, 1996). There are remaining churches in Franklin, Virginia; Ashtabula, Ohio; Baltimore, Maryland; and Washington, DC, that still maintain affiliation with this Seymour-formed group (Dupree, 1996). The headquarters is in Franklin, Virginia, headed by Bishop Stephen Douglas Willis. The group is now called the Apostolic Faith Churches of God, Inc. (AFCOG). These churches developed under the leadership of William J. Seymour. Bishop Seymour came to the Virginia area for the first time in 1909. After starting the work he left Charles Lowe in charge. Lowe split from the group in 1946, and started The Apostolic Faith Church of God and True Holiness (Dupree, 1996). The Franklin church is today led by the aged Bishop D.O. Keyes, who lives in Jefferson, Ohio. He took charge of the work in 1987, becoming its third pastor. Bishop Keyes went to Los Angeles in 1987 and put a tombstone on the grave of William Seymour.

The Final Blow

In 1913 the final blow fell on Seymour's Azusa Street Mission. At a 1913 Pentecostal camp-meeting outside of Los Angeles, the doctrine of the Trinity came under attack. As a result, over 300 people, including all of the Blacks (many of whom were regular attendees at Azusa) accepted the new non-Trinitarian theology. Almost overnight Seymour's following in Los Angeles was reduced to about 20 people.

Maria Woodworth-Etter was the well known evangelist who ran the meeting in Secco Arroyo, California, where the doctrine of Jesus Only was first preached. This picture comes from *A Diary of Signs and Wonders* by Maria Woodworth-Etter, circa 1916.

R. J. Scott led in the planning of the 1915 camp-meeting at Arroyo Seco, California, just outside of Los Angeles. The famous faith healer, Maria Woodworth-Etter, was invited to speak. It is said that William Seymour attended the meeting, but only as a spectator (Martin, 1999). The meeting, well attended, was very spiritual, with many being healed and saved. It was during a baptismal service in which the Canadian R. A. McAlister was invited to teach. Mr. McAlister advocated using the baptismal formula in the "name of Jesus" as opposed to the words, "Father, Son and Holy Ghost" (Foster, 1965; Martin, 1999; Golder, 1973; Brumback, 1961). He even claimed that the words, "Father, Son and Holy Ghost" were never used by the early Church in Christian baptism" (Martin, 1999).

After meditating on McAlister's remarks, throughout the night, John G. Sheppe ran through the camp the next morning, declaring that God had given him the revelation that only the Name of Jesus was to be used in the administration of baptism (Brumback, 1961; Foster, 1965; Golder, 1973; Martin, 1999).

Frank Ewart, Glenn Cook and other Azusa Street veterans quickly developed the idea of re-baptizing in the Name of Jesus. They traveled the country preaching this new doctrine. Immediately G. T. Haywood in Indianapolis re-baptized his entire congregation of 465 in the Name of Jesus (Golder, 1973). The die had been cast. Within a year the Pentecostal movement, which had just been hit by the 1911 doctrinal dispute over salvation, was again rocked with controversy between the trinitarians and the new oneness faction within the movement. Many leaders in the movement were swept along by the "Jesus Only" (Oneness) teaching. Seymour and Parham bitterly fought the new revelation. They reconciled their teaching as the renewal of Sabellianism or Modal Monarchianism, both doctrines which the Fourth Century Christian Church had condemned as heresy.

The core of oneness theology is the belief that God has revealed Himself through His name. The name is God's method of revealing his character and presence. The "personhood" of God is known through the revelation of His name. There is no trinity,

Canadian R. E. McAlister. It was his revelation of the importance of the Name of Jesus for a baptismal formula which caused the great controversy which would split the Pentecostal Movement. This portrait appears in *The Life and Ministry of William J. Seymour* **by Larry Martin.**

but the three-fold divine reality is defined as "three manifestations" of the one spirit that is embodied in the person of Jesus.

Responding to the many doctrinal crises that were beginning to emerge, the Assemblies of God was founded in 1914 in Hot Springs, Arkansas. Its goal was to consider ways of unifying the work of the Pentecostal movement and to deal with common problems. It would not only divide the races, but also end the reign of the Azusa Street Mission as the center of the Pentecostal Movement. Although Larry Martin reports that the Black minister, C.H. Mason, attended and spoke at this meeting (Martin, 1999), it is clear that the group would be an all-white denomination, which it virtually remains to this day.

In 1915 William Seymour wrote a handbook, *The Doctrine and Discipline*, to guide his fledgling organizations. He spent the last days of his life traveling around the country, speaking to mostly African-American churches. He now was called Bishop William J. Seymour (an honorary title he later received, probably from his congregation).

His Death

On September 28, 1922, William suffered a heart attack. Later that same day, around 3:00 PM, he suffered a second one. He was dead at fifty-two years of age. On October 2nd he was buried in a simple casket and wooden vault. Later he would be reburied in a concrete vault when some money had been raised for that purpose.[35] A simple stone was placed at the head of his grave. It was later replaced by D.O. Keyes, pastor of Seymour's Franklin, VA church, with a more elaborate granite one in 1987.[36]

The End of the Azusa Street Mission

After William's death, his wife, Jennie Evans Moore became the leader of what was left of the movement he had founded. Her work ran smoothly until 1930, when remaining members of the Azusa church attempted to wrestle the leadership from her. In 1931 the courts padlocked the building until a court could decide its leadership (Dupree, 1996). Mother Seymour won permission

G.T. Haywood, a founder of the Pentecostal Assemblies of the World. He was one of the first Pentecostals to accept the "new issue". He re-baptized his entire Indianapolis church. This picture taken from, *Before I Sleep* by James L. Tyson.

Andrew David Urshan, an early leader in the Oneness movement, circa 1934. This picture appears in *The Life of Andrew Bar David Urshan*, Apostolic Press, Stockton, California, 1967.

Formal picture of William Seymour, circa 1915. It appears in Douglas Nelson's dissertation, "For Such A Time As This".

Later view of the Azusa Street Mission, circa 1928.

The grave site of William J. Seymour, Evergreen Cemetery in Los Angeles, California, circa 1997. This photo is part of the Rufus Sanders collection.

The last known photograph of William J. Seymour, circa 1922. This photo appears in "For Such A Time As This" by Douglas Nelson.

to continue to lead the Mission through court order. She died on July 7, 1936. She was 62 years old. The building was lost in 1938. The work at Azusa Street was discontinued.

The Mission on Azusa Street was torn down after the Assemblies of God, a direct descendant of the Azusa movement, showed no interest in acquiring it. It was turned into a parking lot, which now makes up the center courtyard of the Japanese-American Culture Center in Los Angeles. The members of the Mission were scattered. The Los Angeles congregation which is the direct descent of the Azusa Street meetings is still active today. It is the Apostolic Faith Home Assembly on 3200 West Adams Boulevard in Los Angeles. The author is proud to say that he has had the opportunity to minister there on numerous occasions over the last 20 years.

Seymour In Perpetuity

The historical memory of Seymour's leadership disappeared, but the fact remains that the Pentecostal/Charismatic renewal movement began among the black people under the leadership of a black man. Because of the tremendous power and appeal generated under Seymour's leadership at the Azusa Street Mission, history cannot erase him. He was one of the most influential black churches leader in American religious history. And because of the twentieth-century worldwide Pentecostal revolution, he is one of the twentieth century's most important religious figures. Pentecostalism has been called the most powerful force within the church at this moment. It is all due to the work of a one-eyed black man named William Joseph Seymour.

AN AFTERWORD

This work has been painstakingly exhausting, but yet a labor of love. It has been about a man who felt a clarion call from God to preach the gospel. To this end he would dedicate his entire adult life. To glimpse Seymour and his vision is to know the tears, pain and indeed the sadness that eludes from the fact that he spent his entire ministry wrestling with problems of human prejudicial inequalities; when he should have been concerned only with the spiritual call of human souls. It is the wounds from that struggle which caused his young death.

Seymour's initial rise to world prominence, as a result of the Azusa Street Revival, has been a long time in coming. It still actually continues to come. It comes unplanned, unrehearsed and without the respect that is due him.

William Seymour was quickly impacted with the same rejection which African-Americans have always known too well in this country. For years his historic, and indeed prophetic contributions to one of the greatest religious movements, since the birth of Christianity, was almost totally ignored.

William J. Seymour's greatness lay not only in the fact that he led the largest religious revival of the twentieth century, but also in his social vision for racial healing. He gave the Christian Church a special chance for racial reconciliation. Tragically though, like his ministry, his vision was ignored. It would not be until the ministry of Martin Luther King, Jr. that the Christian Church would get that opportunity again.

There still is work to be done in the study of the life of William J. Seymour. He yet must be raised to the same folklore status enjoyed by such religious leaders as John Wesley, Richard Allen, Charles Finney or Billy Sunday. His thoughts of social theology still must be looked at with the sensitivity of a visionary who sees things not as they are, but as they should be. The research on his life must not stop until every Christian in America is aware of the man who changed the face of the Christian Church forever. It must not stop until the world knows this Black man who started the twentieth-century Pentecostal movement.

Rufus G.W. Sanders
Hilton Head Island
August 24, 2000

BIBLIOGRAPHY

Adams, M. (1996, March). *Hope in the Midst of Hurt: Towards a Pentecostal Theology of Suffering.* Paper presented at the 25th Anniversary meeting of the Society for Pentecostal Studies, Toronto, Ontario, Canada.

Anderson, R.M. (1979). *Vision of the Disinherited: The Making of American Pentecostalism.* New York, NY: Oxford University Press.

Armstrong, Louis (1954). *Satchmo: My Life in New Orleans.* New York, NY.

Baker, V. (1982). *Louisiana Tapestry: The Ethnic Weave of St. Landry Parish.* Lafayette, Louisiana: University of Southwestern Louisiana Press.

Barboza, Steve. *American Triad: Islam After Malcolm X.* New York, 1993.

Barrett, D.B. (1970). "A.D. 2,000: 350 million Christians in Africa." *International Review of Mission*, 59,233.

Barrett, D.B. (1988). A survey of the twentieth-century Pentecostal/Charismatic renewal in the Holy Spirit, with its goal of world evangelization. In S.M. Burgess, G.B. McGee & P.H. Alexander (Eds.), *Dictionary of Pentecostal and Charismatic Movements.* Grand Rapids, MI: Zondervan Publishing House.

Bartleman, Frank: *Azusa Street: The Roots of Modern-day Pentecost.* Plainfield, NJ: Logos International, 1980.

Bennett, Lerone (1999). *Forced Into Glory Abraham Lincoln's White Dream.* Chicago; Johnson Publishing Co.

Bergerie, M. (1962). *They Tasted Bayou Water: A Brief History of Iberia Parish.* New Orleans: Pelican Publishing Co.

Berry, Fred. *Connections: Leadership Development in Inter-Ethnic Relations*: Los Angeles, Joshua Ministries, 1995.

Blockson, C. (1977). *Black Genealogy.* Baltimore, MD: Black Classic Press.

Broussard, B. (1955). *History of St. Mary Parish.* Franklin, Louisiana.

Brown, Virginia (1981). *Toting the Lead Row: Ruby Pickens Tartt, Alabama Folklorist*. University Press, Alabama.

Brumback, C. (1961). *Life a River: The Early Years of the Assemblies of God*. Springfield, MO: Gospel Publishing House.

Burgess, S.M., McGee, G.B. & Alexander, P.H. (Eds.) (1988). *Dictionary of Pentecostal and Charismatic Movement*. Grand Rapids, MI: Zondervan Publishing House.

Butler, A. (1994, November). *Walls of Division: Racism's Role in Pentecostal History*. Paper presented at the 24th Annual Meeting of the Society of Pentecostal Studies, Wheaton, IL.

Byers, A.L., Birth of a Reformation: Life and Labor of D.S. Warner: Guthrie, Oklahoma. Faith Publishing House, 1966.

Camacho, H. (1986, November). *Historical Roots of Modern Pentecostal Churches: Implications for the Christian Faith*. Paper presented at the annual meeting of the Society for Pentecostal Studies.

Chambers, H. (1925). *A History of Louisiana*. Chicago: The American Historical Society, Inc.

Clemmons, I. (1981, November). *True Koinonia: Pentecostal Hopes and Historical Realities*. Paper presented at the 11th Annual Meeting of the Society for Pentecostal Studies, Charlotte, NC.

Clemmons, Ithiel C., "Charles Harrison Mason," in *Dictionary of Pentecostal and Charismatic Movements*, ed. Stanley M. Burgess and Gary B. McGee; Grand Rapids, Mich.: Zandervan, 1988, 587.

Clemmons, Ithiel, (1981). The Eleventh Annual Meeting of the Society for Pentecostal Studies; Presidential Address, Nov. 12, 1981.

Conrad, G. (1979). *New Iberia: Essays on the Town and Its People*. Lafayette, Louisiana: University of Southwestern Louisiana Press.

Daniels, W.H. (1877). *Moody: His Word, Work and Workers*. New York, NY: Hitchcock and Walden.

Davis, C. (1983). *Azusa Street 'Til Now: Eyewitness Accounts of the Move of God*. Tulsa, OK: Harrison House.

Dayton, D. (1987). *Theological Roots of Pentecostalism*. Metuchen, NJ: Scarecrow Press, Inc.

DuBois, W.E.B. (1903). *The Negro Chronicles*. Atlanta: Atlanta University Press.

DuBois, W.E.B. (1969). *The Souls of Black Folk*. New York, NY: Signet Classic.

Dupree, Sherry. *African-American Holiness Pentecostal Movement: An Annotated Bibliography*. New York City: Garland Publishing, Inc., 1996.

Dupree, Sherry, (1996). *African-American Holiness Pentecostal Movement*, (Garland Publishing, New York).

Elbert, P. (1988). *Faces of Renewal*. Peabody, MD: Hendrickson Publishing.

Ewart, Frank (1975). *The Phenomenon of Pentecost*, Pentecostal Publishing House, Hazelwood, MO.

Faupel, D.W. (1992). *Whither Pentecostalism?* 22nd Presidential Address at the Society for Pentecostal Studies.

Faupel D.W. (1993). *Whither Pentecostalism? Pneuma: The Journal of the Society for Pentecostal Studies*. 15(1), 9-27.

Fisher, M. (1953). *Negro Slave Songs in the United States*. Ithaca, NY: Cornell University Press.

Fortier, A. (1909). *Louisiana*. Atlanta: Southern Historical Association.

Foster, F. (1965). *Think It Not Strange: A History of the Oneness Movement*. St. Louis, MO: Pentecostal Publishing House.

Foster, Fred J. Their Story: Twentieth-Century Pentecostals: Hazelwood, MO: World Aflame Press, 1965.

Gadsen, Sam (1974). *An Oral History of Edisto Island: Sam Gadsen Tells the Story*. Geshen, IN.

Gee, D. (1967). *Wind and Flame*. Nottingham, England: Assemblies of God Publishing House.

Ginzburg, R. (1962). *100 Years of Lynchings*. Baltimore, MD: Black Classic Press.

Guirard, L. (1950). *St. Martinville: The Land of Evangeline in Picture Story*. St. Martinville, LA: City Press

Goff, James (1988). *Fields White Unto Harvest: Charles F. Parham and the Missionary Origins of Pentecostalism*, Fayetteville: University of Arkansas Press.

Golder, M. (1973). *History of the Pentecostal Assemblies of the World*. Indianapolis, IN: Pentecostal Assemblies of the World, Inc.

Hamilton, C.V. (1972). *The Black Preacher in America*. New York, NY: William Morrow & Company, Inc.

Harlon, Louis, (Ed.)(1972-89). *The Booker T. Washington Papers* (14 Vols.). New York, NY.

Henry, H. (1970). "Toward a Religion of Revolution." *The Black Scholar*. 2(4), 27-31.

Hill, Ruth, (Ed.)(199). *The Black Women Oral History Project* (10 Vols.; Westport, CT), Vol. 23.

Hollenweger, W.J. (1970). *Black Pentecostal Concept*. Birmingham, England: University of Birmingham.

Hollenweger, W.J. (1972). *The Pentecostals*. Minneapolis, MN: Augsburg Publishing House.

Holsey, Albon (April 1929). "Learning How to Be Black." *American Mercury XVI*, 421-25.

Horton, S.M. (Ed.) (1994). *Systematic Theology*. Springfield, MO: Logion Press.

Hudson, Hosea (1972). *Black Worker in the Deep South: A Personal Account*. New York, NY.

Johns, C.B. (1995). "The Adolescence of Pentecostalism: In Search of a Legitimate Sectarian Identity." *Pneuma: The Journal of the Society of Pentecostal Studies*. 17(1), 3-17.

Johnson, Charles (1941). "These Are Our Lives." *Federal Writers' Project*. Washington, DC.

Johnson James, (1933). *The Autobiography of James Weldon Johnson*. New York, NY.

Jones, T. (1991). *The Civil War Memoirs of Captain William J. Seymour: Reminiscences of a Louisiana Tiger*. Baton Rouge: Baton Rouge, Louisiana State University Press.

Kantzer, K.S. (1980). "The Charismatic Among Us." *Christianity Today*.

Kelsey, Morton. *Tongue Speaking: An Experiment in Spiritual Experience*, Garden City, N.Y.; Doubleday, 1964.

Kramer, Jean T. (1982). *Louisiana Tapestry: The Ethnic Weave of St. Landry Parish*. Lafayette, Louisiana: University of Southwestern Louisiana Press.

Litwack, Leon (1979). *Been in the Storm So Long: The Aftermath of Slavery*. New York, NY: Alfred A. Knopf Publishing.

Litwack, Leon (1998). *Trouble In Mind: Black Southerners in the Age of Jim Crow*. New York, NY: Alfred A. Knopf Publishing.

Levering, Lewis. *W.E.B. DuBois: Biography of A Race*. New York, 1993.

Lewis, C.S. (1943). *Mere Christianity*. New York, NY: MacMillan Publishing Company.

Locke Audrey (1911). *The Seymour Family: History and Romance*. London: Constable and Company, Ltd.

Los Angeles Daily Times, Wednesday morning, 19 April 1906, Part 11, p. 1. Text reproduced in Nelson dissertation, pp. 313-4.

Lovell, J. (1939). "The Social Implications of The Negro Spiritual." *Journal of Negro Education*, Oct. 1939, 634-43.

Lovett, L. (1978). *Black Holiness-Pentecostalism: Implications for Ethics and Social Transformation*. Unpublished doctoral dissertation, Atlanta, GA: Emory University.

MacRoberts, Iain, (1988). *The Black Roots and White Racism of Early Pentecostalism In The USA*, (MacMillan Press, London, 1988).

Marshall, C. (1970). "The Black Church Its Mission is Liberation." *The Black Scholar*. 2(4), 13-19.

Martin, Larry (1999). *The Life and Ministry of William J. Seymour and a History of the Azusa Street Revival*. Joplin, Missouri: Christian Life Books.

Mays, Benjamin (1971). *Born to Rebel: An Autobiography*. New York, NY.

McDonnell, K. (1995). "Improbable Conversations: The International Classical Pentecostal/Roman Catholic Dialogue." *Pneuma: The Journal of the Society for Pentecostal Studies*. 17(2), 163-188.

Menzies, W.W. and Horton, S.M. (Eds.) (1993). *Bible Doctrines: A Pentecostal Perspective*. Springfield, MO: Logion Press.

Montgomery, W. (1995). *Under Their Own Vine and Fig Tree: The African-American Church in the South 1865-1900*. Baton Rouge: Louisiana University Press.

Montgomery, William E. *Under their own Vine and Fig Tree: The African-American Church in the South 1865-1900*. Baton Rouge: Louisiana State University Press, 1989.

Montgomery, William E. *Under Their Own Vine and Fig Tree: The African-American Church in the South 1865-1900*. Baton Rouge: Louisiana University Press, 1993.

Moses, Wilson. *The Golden Age of Black Nationalism*. 1850-1925, Hamden, Connecticut, 1978.

Morton, Robert (1922). *Finding a Way Out: An Autobiography*. New York, NY: Alfred A. Knopf Publishing.

Murphy, M. (Ed.)(1993). *Encyclopedia of African-American Religions*. New York: Garland Publishing, Inc.

Murray, Pamli (1956). *The Story of An American Family*. New York, NY: Alfred A. Knopf Publishing.

Nelson, D.J. (1981). *For Such A Time As This: The Study of Bishop William J. Seymour and the Azusa Street Revival*. Unpublished doctoral dissertation, University of Birmingham, England.

Nichol, J.T. (1966). *The Pentecostals*. Plainfield, NJ: Logos International.

Nickel, T. (1979). *Azusa Street Outpouring*. Hanford, CA: Great Commission International.

Parham, C.F. (1912, December). "Apostolic Faith." In A. Butler (Ed.) (1994). *Walls of Division: Racism's Role in Pentecostal History*. Paper presented at the 24th Annual Meeting of the Society for Pentecostal Studies, Wheaton, IL.

Parham, Charles (1944). *A Voice Crying In The Wilderness*, Joplin Printing Co., Baxter Springs, Kansas.

Paris, A.E. (1982). *Black Pentecostalism: Southern Religion in an Urban World*. Amherst, MA: The University of Massachusetts Press.

Perrin, W. (1891). *Southwest Louisiana Biographical and Historical*. New Orleans: The Gulf Publishing Company.

Perdue, Charles (1976); (Ed.) *Weevils in Wheat: Interviews with Virginia Ex- Slaves*. Charlottesville, VA: Alfred A. Knopf Publishing.

Pharr Chamber of Commerce, Valley Internet Services, 1998.

Pharr, H.N. (1955). *Pharrs and Farrs With Other Descendants From Five Scotch-Irish Pioneers In America*. Ann Arbor, MI: Edward Brothers, Inc.

Pinder, K. (1997). Images of Christ in African American Painting. *African American Review*. 31(2), 223-232.

Quarels, B. (1969). *Black Abolitionists*. New York, NY: Plenum Publishing Corporation.

Quebedeaux, R. (1976). *The New Charismatics: The Origins, Development and Significance of Neo-Pentecostalism*. New York,

NY: Doubleday.

Raboteau, A.J. (1997). *A Fire In the Bones: Reflections on African-American Religious History*. Boston: Beacon Press.

Raboteau, A.J. (1997). *African American Religion: Interpretive Essays in History and Cultures*. New York, NY: Routledge.

Redkey, E.S. (1969). *Black Exodus: Black Nationalist Movements, 1890-1910*. New Haven, CT: Yale University Press.

Redkey, Edwin. *Black Exodus, Black Nationalist and Back-to-Africa Movements*, 1890-1910, New Haven, 1969.

Richardson, J. (1980). *With Water and Spirit: A History of Black Apostolic Denominations in the U.S.* Washington, DC: Spirit Press.

Riggs, R.M. (1949). *The Spirit Himself*. Springfield, MO: Gospel Publishing House.

Riley, Clayton (1980). *Daddy King: An Autobiography*. New York, NY: Knopf Publishing.

Robeck, C.M. (1993). "Taking Stock of Pentecostalism: The Personal Reflections of a Retiring Editor." *Pneuma: The Journal of the Society of Pentecostal Studies*. 15(1), 35-60.

Robeck, Cecil M. (1998). William J. Seymour: The Formation of a Pentecostal Leader, Pasadena, California, unpublished paper.

Robinson, James (1950). *Road Without Turning: The Story of Reverend James H. Robinson: An Autobiography*. New York, NY: Knopf Publishing.

Robinson, S.B. (1997). *The Pursuit of His Glory: Maturing in the Image of Christ*, Shippenburg, PA: Destiny Image Publishers.

Robinson, S.B. (1997, March). *Beyond the Five-fold Gospel: In Pursuit of a Pentecostal Mandate for the 21st Century*. Paper presented at the 27th Annual Meeting of the Society for Pentecostal Studies, Oakland, CA.

Rooks, C.S. (1990). *Revolution in Zion: Reshaping African American Ministry, 1960-1974*. New York, NY: Pilgrim Press.

Sanders, Cheryl. Saints In Exile. New York: Oxford University Press, 1996.

Seymour, Malcolm (1982). *Puritan Migration to Connecticut: Saga of the Seymour Family 1129-1746*. Canaan, New Hampshire: The Phoenix Publishing Company.

Shumway (1919). Charles William, "A Critical History of Glossolalia," Ph.D diss., Boston University.

Singleton, Gregory H. (1977). *Religion in the City of Angels.* (UMI Research Press), Ann Arbor.

Spratling, W. (1927). *Old Plantation Houses in Louisiana.* New York: Lent & Groff Co.

Stahls, P. (1979). *Plantation Homes of the Teche Country.* New Orleans: Pelican Publishing Co.

Synan, V. (1975). *Aspects of Pentecostal--Charismatic Origins.* Plainfield, NJ: Logos International.

Synan, H. Vinson, "William Joseph Seymour," in Burgess and McGee, *Dictionary,* ed. 780.

Synan, Vinson. *The Holiness Pentecostal Movement.* Grand Rapids: William B. Eurdmars Publishing Co., 1971.

Synan, Vinson. (Editor) *Aspects of Pentecostal-Charismatic Origins,* Plainfield, New Jersey: Logos International, 1975.

Taylor, C. (1994). *The Black Churches of Brooklyn.* New York, NY: Columbia University Press.

Terrell, Mary (1940). *A Colored Woman in a White World.* Washington, DC: Alfred A. Knopf Publishing.

Tinney, J. (1971, October 8). "Black Origins of the Pentecostal Movement." *Christianity Today,* 4-6.

Tinney, J. (1976). *Essays Commemorating the Dedication of Seymour House at Howard University.* Washington, DC: Spirit Press.

Tinney, J. (1978, December). *Exclusivist Tendencies in Pentecostal Self-Definitions.* Paper presented at the meeting of the Society for Pentecostal Studies.

Tinney, James S. *In The Tradition of William J. Seymour.* Essays commemorating the dedication of Seymour House at Howard University, Washington, D.C. Spirit Press, 1978.

Tinney, James S. "A Theoretical and Historical Comparison of Black Political and Religious Movements" (Ph.D. dissertation, Howard University, 1978).

Tinney, James S. "William J. Seymour" Father of Modern-day Pentecostalism" in *Black Apostles,* ed. Randall K. Burkett and Richard Newman: Boston: G.K. Hall, 1978; 217

Tinney, James S. "The Blackness of Pentecostalism, *Spirit* 3, No. 2 (1979).

Turner, William C., Jr., "Movements in the Spirit: A Review of African-American Holiness/Pentecostal/Apostolics," in Directory of African-American Religious Bodies, ed. Wardell Payne: Washington, D.C., Howard University Press, 1991, 250.

Tyson, J. (Ed.)(1990). *Chalices of Gold: A Narrative and Pictorial History of the Pentecostal Assembly of the World*. (Vols. 1-7). Warren, OH: Tyson Publishing.

Van Dusen, H.P. (1958, June 9). "The Third Force in Christendom: Force's Lessons for Others." *Life*, 122-123.

Washington, Booker T. (1901). *Up From Slavery: An Autobiography*. New York, NY.

Washington, Booker T. (1909). *The Rise of the Race from Slavery* (2 Vols.). New York, NY.

Washington, J.M. (1986). *Frustrated Fellowship: The Black Baptist Quest for Social Power*. Macon, GA: Mercer University Press.

Wharton, Lane (1947). *The Negro In Mississippi, 1865-1890*, Chapel Hill: Wake Forest Press.

Wilmore, Gayrand S., *Black Religion and Black Radicalism*. Mary Knoll, New York, 1973, p. 41.

Woodward, C. Van (1951). *Origins of the New South*, Oxford: Oxford University Press.

Woodward, C. Van (1966). *The Strange Career of Jim Crow*, Oxford: Oxford University Press.

Wright, Richard (1945). *Black Boy: A Record of Childhood and Youth*. New York, NY: Alfred A. Knopf Publishing.

Wright, Richard (1965). *87 Years Behind the Black Curtain: An Autobiography*. Philadelphia, PA: Alfred A. Knopf Publishing.

Notes

[1] Usually, but not exclusively, the religious phenomenon of making sounds that constitute, or resemble, a language not known to the speaker, referred to as speaking in tongues.

[2] Van Dusen wrote in *Life* magazine on the *Third Force in Christendom*, June 9, 1958. He called Pentecostalism "The Third Force."

[3] Van Dusen referred to first and second forces as being Catholicism and Protestantism, respectively in his June 9, 1958 article for *Life* magazine entitled, "The Third Force in Christendom: Force's Lessons for Others."

[4] I believe that had Professor Tinney lived (he died at a rather young age in 1978), he would have completed a biography of the "Father of Pentecostalism."

[5] The Great Commission is the message given to the disciples by Christ and it is the foundation for Christian proselytizing of the world found in St. Matthew 28:19.

[6] Pentecost refers to the Jewish holiday that follows by fifty days the Christian Resurrection of Jesus Christ. It was for the Jews the celebration of Passover. For Christians it was the official day on which the Christian Church begins as recorded in Acts 2:38.

[7] The author traveled this route to see the remaining effects of St. Mary Parish. Much of this information can be obtained from reading any geographical guide of the area.

[8] USA Today, Friday, Feb. 26, 1999. Destinations & Diversions. Section D.

[9] This information taken from official Census records of St. Mary Parish, Louisiana; housed in the New Orleans City library. New Orleans, Louisiana.

[10] Taken from the Department of Commerce, Bureau of Census, 1880; St. Mary Parish, Marriage Records, July 26, 1867.

[11] *Ibid.*

[12] *Ibid.*

[13] *Ibid.*

[14] This story was told to the author while researching at the Amistad Center at Tulane University in New Orleans (10/11/98).

[15] Horatio Seymour, like all American Seymours, was a descendant of Richard Seymour, who had emigrated from Hertfordshire England to America in 1638 as part of the great Puritan Migration led by Thomas Hooker, founder of the Connecticut Colony (Seymour, 1982). These Seymours were the last of the Hooker contingent to leave England and to join in the already established community of Hartford (Seymour, 1982). The Seymours, along with the Steeles, Talcotts, Marrus, Ruscols and Websters who preceded them, through intermarriages would create what would become Colonial America (Seymour, 1991).

The Seymours trace their heritage all the way back to the 7th Century and the Village of Touraine, St. Maur Sur-Loire (Locke, 1911). This all before William the Conqueror began uniting the English. The Seymours, as the St. Maur family was originally known, takes its name from a certain black hermit called St. Maur or Mauras (Locke, 1911).

Upon arrival in America the Seymours helped to complete the building of Hartford and went on to build Norwalk, Connecticut. They moved down the eastern seaboard settling in every colony. Today many towns throughout this country bear their name, *i.e.*, Seymour, Indiana; Seymour, Louisiana; Seymour, Connecticut.

[16] For accounts of this event, see The New Orleans Daily Picayne, Nov. 2, 3, 4, 1884 and The New Orleans Times-Democrat, Nov. 2, 3, 4, 1884. Both are reported in Glenn R. Conrad's *New Iberia Essays On The Town and Its People.*

[17] *Ibid.*

[18] Wright, Richard (1945). *Black Boy: A Record of Childhood and Youth*, New York, New York; and Wright, Richard (1965) *Years Behind the Black Curtain: An Autobiography*, Philadelphia, PA.

[19] The Republican-populist movement was an insurgency movement against the Democratic oligarchy in the post-reconstruction South.

[20] Observation recorded by Douglas Nelson in his dissertation, "For Such A Time As This," p.

[21] Evening Light is a term associated with the Church of God reformation movement. These people assumed an identity with reference to Zec. 14:7 (King James Version).

[22] This information was provided in a conversation with Cecil M. Robeck, professor at Fuller Theological Seminary, and can be found in his unpublished manuscript, William J. Seymour: The Formation of a Pentecostal Leader, made available to the author.

[23] As cited on page 165 of Nelson's unpublished dissertation, "For Such a Time As This, The Story of Bishop William J. Seymour and the Azusa Street Revival." It is reported in the "Weird Babel of Tongues" articles that William J. Seymour had a glass eye.

[24] The American Colonization Society was founded in 1817. It advocated overseas colonization for freed black slaves. It was responsible for the creation of Liberia in West Africa; America's only established colony.

[25] Bobby Vaughn's web-site address is http://www.stanford.edu/~bvaugn.

[26] Author's conversation with Bobby Vaughn, anthropologist, Stanford University, about Afro-Mexican history. 2/3/2000.

[27] Mel Robeck, Professor of Church History at Fuller Theological Seminary, Pasadena, and personal friend of author, provided this information in conversations and in an unpublished paper given to author during a 1999 Los Angeles visit.

[28] Acts 2:4 -- is the standard verse used by Pentecostals to verify the speaking in tongues as accepted Christian doctrine.

[29] As seen in any number of remaining photos of the house and as seen by the author on numerous research trips to Bonnie Brae Street in Los Angeles.

[30] The third blessing refers to speaking in tongues. The first blessing was salvation. The second blessing refers to sanctification.

[31] This was also told to author as one of the many stories of folklore that attends the Azusa Street Story. The original piano, though, still sits in the House on Bonnie Brae Street.

[32] The information in this section was gathered from several interviews with Mel Robeck, professor at Fuller Theological Seminary, as well as an article by Bob Pool that appeared in the Los Angeles Times, Jan. 18, 1991, and from several conversations while the author was conducting research in Los Angeles in April, 1999.

[33] Information about the physical condition of the church is taken from a paper by Pentecostal expert, Douglas J. Nelson, "The Black Face of Church Renewal"; unpublished paper, 1980 (Library of Rufus G.W. Sanders).

[34] Upper room refers to the upstairs dwelling where the Spirit fell on the disciples of Christ on The Feast of Pentecost in Acts, second chapter (King James Version).

[35] The author talked with Keyes who is in his late 80's. He lives in Jefferson, Ohio. The conversation took place on 7/6/97 via telephone.

[36] The author visited the grave site at Evergreen Cemetery in 1997 and saw the burial records and viewed the grave.

CPSIA information can be obtained at www.ICGtesting.com
Printed in the USA
LVOW051535130612

285953LV00001B/271/A